WHEN ORDINARY MEETS
Extraordinary

Walk in the footsteps of
those who experienced the arrival of
the greatest Gift ever given.

Mark D. Fortney

PR8:2
Books

Unless otherwise indicated, Scripture quotations taken from THE HOLY BIBLE, NEW INTERNATIONAL VERSION®. Copyright © 1973, 1978, 1984 by International Bible Society. Used with permission.

Scripture quotations marked ESV are taken from The ESV® Bible (The Holy Bible, English Standard Version®), copyright © 2001 by Crossway, a publishing ministry of Good News Publishers. Used by permission. All rights reserved.

Scripture references marked MSG are taken from THE MESSAGE. Copyright © 1993, 1994, 1995, 1996, 2000, 2001, 2002. Used by permission of NavPress Publishing Group.

Scripture quotations marked NASB are taken from the *New American Standard Bible®*, Copyright © 1960, 1971, 1977, 1995 by The Lockman Foundation. Used by permission.

Scripture quotations marked NLT are taken from the *Holy Bible, New Living Translation*, copyright ©1996, 2004, 2015 by Tyndale House Foundation. Used by permission of Tyndale House Publishers, Carol Stream, Illinois 60188. All rights reserved.

Printed in the United States of America | First Edition (November 2023)

Cover Art: David Litwin (purefusionmedia.com)

ISBN: 979-8-9893709-0-0 (international trade paper edition)

Library of Congress Control Number: 2023920431

For permission requests, bulk church group orders, or speaking inquiries, please contact the author at mark@thefortneys.com.

Contents

To Lisa, my loving wife,
who humors my child-like enthusiasm for Christmas
by putting up Christmas decorations early
and taking them down late.

PART I

Before the Arrival

1

Prelude: Christmas Is Coming

Christmas is my favorite time of year. I love it! It's been that way as far back as I can remember. I love the music! I love the decorations (although maybe not the decorating)! I love the cookies! I even enjoy the shopping. And when I was a child, I loved the presents—especially the presents—both giving and receiving.

During my middle school years, I was a paperboy for the local evening paper, the *Pittsburgh Press*. I'd get home from school and go out to deliver papers to my neighbors. Every week I'd also knock on their doors to collect the money they owed for that week's paper subscription. Tipping was a big part of my pay, especially at Christmastime. During an average Christmas season, I'd get $250 in tips. That was a lot of money for an eleven-year-old!

So what did I do with that extra money? Every year, I spent it on three Christmas gifts: one gift for my parents, one for my sister, and one for my brother. For the Christmas of 1976, I bought my parents the best Christmas present my young mind could imagine...the coolest lava lamp ever!

That Christmas morning, my parents opened the gift with all the gratitude they could muster. Mom and I went upstairs to their bedroom and plugged in the lava lamp, right where it could be easily seen.

The following Monday, I noticed that the lava lamp was gone. "It stopped working," was Mom's explanation. "So, I boxed it up to return." I didn't think too much about it.

A week later, I asked Mom where the replacement lava lamp was. "It was such a popular gift that they were out of stock," she replied. "So, we'll keep checking back."

About three years later, it hit me: The lava lamp was never replaced, and it never would be. But somehow, Mom still made the gift-giver feel appreciated, even if the gift itself was not.

Reflecting on those years, Advent was a big part of my Christmas experience, serving as a sort of countdown clock. I loved to count off the passing Sundays, as a new candle was lit. Four Sundays, then Christmas morning and—no, not celebrating Jesus' birth—opening presents! The anticipation would build to a feverish pitch. And by the time Christmas Eve arrived, who could sleep?

Years passed, and I grew up. I finally realized the emptiness of my previous understanding of this most precious

Season. I longed to get beyond plastic manger scenes and presents, recapturing the underlying truth. I marveled that God would come to live among us, born into such humble circumstances. I was in awe of the fact that birth looked so ordinary, yet so different for Jesus. And did I mention that our Savior would one day return? Amazing stuff!

Advent is both much older and more meaningful than I ever understood as a child. It is a Latin word meaning "the arrival." As early as the fourth century, believers set aside the weeks before Christmas to celebrate Jesus' birth but also to long for His return. So Advent is a season characterized by many emotions, including anticipation, hope, and joy.

Ironically, as a child, I got at least some emotions of Advent right. I experienced anticipation and hope when contemplating the soon-to-arrive present-giving-and-receiving. The only problem was that the gift I was anticipating was not the ultimate Gift, the One who loves us selflessly and will come again! In short, as a child I was focused on presents and missed the real Gift, Jesus.

I was not—and will not be—the last person to miss the real reason for the Christmas Season. In fact, you don't have to look any further than the Bible for stories of ordinary people who were surprised by their encounter with this extraordinary Child.

When Ordinary Meets Extraordinary will examine the lives of ordinary people as they encounter the infinite, the perfect, the extraordinary incarnate God, born to a humble girl. We'll explore their responses as they encounter the reality of the Messiah's arrival—before, during, and after—while focusing on Mary, Joseph, the Shepherds, Simeon, and the Wise Men.

However, my desire in authoring this book is to encourage you to thoughtfully consider your own response to an encounter with the extraordinary Jesus. Many of us risk exchanging the Extraordinary for the ordinary when we take our Christmas cues from the broader culture. So, after each chapter, you'll find a few questions for reflection.

> Many exchange the Extraordinary for the ordinary when taking Christmas cues from the broader culture.

I firmly believe that how you respond to Jesus will have the single most important impact on your life today, tomorrow, and for all eternity. I can think of no better way to gain a new perspective on the Christmas Season than to walk in the footsteps of those who experienced Jesus' coming firsthand.

Personal Study: Going Deeper

What does it mean to you that the Son of God came into this world as a baby, in the humblest of circumstances?

- What does this teach us about God?
- What does it say about your worth to God?

What are some important ways that the Christ-Child has impacted you?

- Are others able to recognize His impact on your life?
- Why might it be important for others to observe this change?

Finally, why should the birth of *Immanuel* ("God with us") be a source of great rejoicing for you during this special season?

2

Mary's Response: Joy

Luke 1:26-49

Like most first-time mothers, Mary must have experienced a wide range of emotions as she awaited the birth of her firstborn, Jesus. From anxiousness to anticipation to joy—and everything in between—life was surely full of ups and downs. But while we can identify with Mary's story in some ways, it's important to remember that in other ways, this birth was unlike any other.

Mary was just an ordinary girl, a teenager of humble means. Yet she would be used in an extraordinary way, as the mother of the long-awaited *Messiah* (Hebrew for "anointed one"). This was a one-of-a-kind event in all of human history! As Scripture tells us, Jesus represented salvation not only for the Jewish people—including Mary—but for all people of all times.

Before examining Mary's story, let's paint a picture of the world into which Mary's Son was born, focusing on the historical, scriptural, and cultural contexts.

Historical Context

If we had access to newspaper headlines in 6 BC, they might have looked something like this:

The Nazareth Daily News

"Emperor Augustus Declares a Census Requiring Return to Ancestral Homes"

"Roman Soldiers Kill 6 Zealots in Clash Outside of Jerusalem"

"King Herod Mandates Significant Tax Increase"

"Unrest with Roman Rule Reaching Record Levels Across Israel"

"A Majority of Jews Surveyed Expect Messiah to Arrive Soon"

Jesus was born into turbulent times. Violence was common. A strong sense of dissatisfaction with the current political environment was palpable. Yet, for some, a profound sense of hopelessness had taken root. The time seemed right for revolution. Something had to change.

The Jews had an unmistakable sense that the Messiah would soon arrive. Many believed He would be a powerful Warrior-King who would throw off the yoke of Roman oppression. He would arrive in a thunder cloud with a sword in His hand. However, this was not what Scripture meant when it said that the Messiah would save His people. He intended to save them from their sin—with eternal ramifications—while the people wanted to be saved from their earthly enemies.

Scriptural Context

The Old Testament is laden with messianic prophecies that can help us better understand what the Jews should have been looking for in a Savior. How would they identify Him when He arrived? Here's a brief overview.

Isaiah 7:14: Therefore the Lord himself will give you a sign: The virgin will be with child and will give birth to a son and will call him Immanuel.

Isaiah 9:6-7: For to us a child is born, to us a son is given, and the government will be on his shoulders. And he will be called Wonderful Counselor, Mighty God, Everlasting Father, Prince of Peace. ... He will reign on David's throne and over his kingdom, establishing and upholding it with justice and righteousness from that time on and forever.

Malachi 3:1: "See, I will send my messenger, who will prepare the way before me. Then suddenly the Lord you are seeking will come to his temple; the messenger of the covenant, whom you desire, will come," says the LORD Almighty.

Micah 5:2: But you, Bethlehem Ephrathah, though you are among the small clans of Judah, out of you will come for me one who will be ruler over Israel, whose origins are from of old, from ancient times.

According to Scripture, the promised Messiah would be a Son born to a virgin. Thus, He would arrive in Bethlehem as a Baby. But this Baby was unlike any seen before or since. He would be called *Immanuel*, which means "God with us." He would be a descendant of King David, ushering in an everlasting kingdom, championing peace and reconciliation. Finally, the Messiah would have a forerunner, John the Baptizer, to announce His coming and prepare the people for His arrival.

Cultural Context

Mary's story is set in a culture different from our own. She faced many challenges as a woman who was pregnant but had not yet finalized her marriage.

Mary was betrothed to Joseph, which was somewhat like an engagement today but legally binding. The betrothal period lasted for one year, during which the couple was known as husband and wife. The differences between betrothal and marriage were twofold: The couple did not live together, and physical intimacy was prohibited.[1]

Because of these norms, pregnancy before marriage brought extreme shame and embarrassment to the future mother, which likely resulted in the entire family being ostracized. Furthermore, if a formal charge of adultery was made, the woman could be stoned, according to Mosaic Law.

If the betrothed husband of the unfaithful woman finalized the marriage, shame and embarrassment would also fall on him. This was not the usual decision of a "righteous man," which is how the Bible described Joseph.[2]

The Setting: Who, What, Where, When

Mary's story is found in Luke. An extraordinary encounter is about to take place, but first the facts are reported in Luke 1:26-27.

> In the sixth month, God sent the angel Gabriel to Nazareth, a town in Galilee, to a virgin pledged [*betrothed*] to be married to a man named Joseph, a descendant of David. The virgin's name was Mary.

Mary was visited by an angel when Elizabeth was six months pregnant. She was Mary's relative and had miraculously conceived a son in her old age.

Gabriel is one of only two angels mentioned by name in Scripture.[3] He is referenced four times, always in relation to bringing an important message from God. *Angels* (literally "messengers") are immortal spirit beings created by God to carry out His will, and there are an exceedingly large number of them.

This extraordinary encounter between Mary and Gabriel took place around Nazareth, which was a small, inconsequential town of a few hundred people. Located about 65 miles due north of Jerusalem[4] in Galilee, Jesus' disciple Nathanael would one day comment: "Can anything good come out of Nazareth?"[5] In other words, this town was nothing special.

So, Mary was an ordinary girl from an unremarkable town. The Greek word used to describe her can be translated as "virgin" or "maiden." Either way, it implies a young female of marriageable age—likely twelve to fourteen years old—who had not had relations with a man. Mary lived with her family and, although she was likely illiterate, she was undoubtedly familiar with the Hebrew Scriptures and the prophecies related to the Messiah.

This story's background would not be complete without a mention of Joseph, Mary's betrothed. He was much older than her, as the husband was expected to be well established and able to support both himself and a wife (and eventually children). Joseph was known as a godly man, descended from King David, who earned a living as a carpenter.

Gabriel's Message

Continuing with Luke 1:28-33, Mary's extraordinary encounter with Gabriel unfolds.

> The angel [*Gabriel*] went to her [*Mary*] and said, "Greetings, you who are highly favored! The Lord is with you." Mary was greatly troubled at his words and wondered what kind of greeting this might be. But the angel said to her, "Do not be afraid, Mary, you have found favor with God. You will be with child and give birth to a son, and you are to give him the name Jesus. He will be great and will be called the Son of the Most High. The Lord God will give him the throne of his father David, and he will reign over the house of Jacob forever; his kingdom will never end."

Mary was initially "confused and disturbed"[6] by this strange angelic encounter. Who could blame her? This kind of thing didn't happen every day. And what had she done to find favor with God? In reality, there was nothing she did to earn it. The Greek word translated "favor" (*charis*) is also translated "grace." And when God extends grace, it is always *unmerited* by definition. So, He chose Mary for this honor. And it would alter her life in a most amazing way!

Gabriel told Mary that she would give birth to a son named *Jesus* (literally "God is salvation"). But not just any son. Gabriel revealed four specific truths about this Son.

He would be great!

He would be called "Son of the Most High." For this special Baby would be like no other, being both fully God and fully Human.

God the Father would give His Son the throne of King David in accordance with biblical prophecy.

And Jesus' reign would not end but go on forever!

Based on this description, Mary understood the angel was speaking about the Messiah's coming. Her Son would be the long-awaited "Anointed One," promised in Scripture so many centuries earlier! But what did Mary think about this extraordinary message? What questions did she have? Picking up with Luke 1:34-37:

"How will this be," Mary asked the angel, "since I am a virgin?" The angel answered, "The Holy Spirit will come upon you, and the power of the Most High will overshadow you. So the holy one to be born will be called the Son of God. Even Elizabeth your relative is going to have a child in her old age, and she who was said to be barren is in her sixth month. For nothing is impossible with God."

Mary was understandably confused and surprised by the angel's message but not for the reason we might expect. She was not surprised that the long-awaited Messiah was finally coming. Rather, Mary was surprised that she—who had never known a man intimately—would be a mother.

Interestingly, Gabriel did not rebuke Mary, since her question was not rooted in unbelief.[7] Rather, Mary was simply wondering how it would be accomplished. As she understood it, there was only one way that babies were made. Gabriel patiently answered Mary's question and explained that the Spirit of God would bring about the physical conception.

As proof that this extraordinary message was true, Gabriel told Mary that the impossible had already happened. Mary's relative, Elizabeth, who was beyond child-bearing years, was already six months pregnant. She would bear a son, John, the one prophesied to prepare the way for the Messiah.[8]

Then, to make his point crystal clear, the angel left Mary with this amazing truth: "Nothing is impossible with God!" For God's Son could and would become flesh—born of a virgin—and dwell among men. Why? Because God could do it and God willed it.

So, God cannot be constrained. As humans, our options are limited, but not God's. He is not finite, but infinite. He is not the created, but the Creator. God is not bound by time and space, nor human biology. So (1) Mary's young age and insignificant social standing were not limitations for God; (2) Mary's betrothal to Joseph did not deter God; and (3) even the laws of nature did not restrict God.

Mary Responds

Initial Response: Obedience

After God's message was delivered and questions were answered, what was Mary's initial response? Let's look at her own words, as recorded in Luke 1:38.

> "I am the Lord's servant," Mary answered. "May it be to me as you have said." Then the angel left her.

Mary's response to this extraordinary...crazy...amazing... mind-blowing...message was obedience. She willingly submitted to God's plan, as His servant. I'm sure it didn't make much sense to her at the time, but Mary trusted God fully and knew that He was capable of doing anything He chose to do.

If you were Mary, do you think you would respond in the same way she did, given the repercussions that would likely follow? Her short answer in the affirmative was both resolute and incredibly brave. For Mary, the only way to respond to God's plan was obedience. She trusted God more than she trusted herself or her fears!

> Obedience should be our default response to God.

Ultimate Response: Joy

In the heat of the moment, Mary responded to God's message with an obedient heart. But after she had some time to think about it, did she have regrets? Did Mary want to back out?

Let's briefly skip ahead several verses and check-in on Mary after her extraordinary encounter with Gabriel. By this time, she had departed for the house of her relative, Elizabeth, to spend three months with her. As they greeted one another, Elizabeth reacted with joy regarding the special nature of Mary's pregnancy.

In Luke 1:46-49, Mary responded to Elizabeth's joy with joy-filled words of her own.

> And Mary said: "My soul glorifies the Lord and my spirit rejoices in God my Savior, for he has been mindful of the humble state of his servant. From now on, all generations will call me blessed, for the Mighty One has done great things for me—holy is his name."

In response to the message Mary received from Gabriel—that she would be the Messiah's mother—she rejoiced, understanding that God's special favor would lead to all generations calling her blessed. She felt this way despite the negative consequences that awaited her in the near term. After all, Mary was still a betrothed girl who was pregnant...and not by the one she was betrothed to!

Yet Mary could still say with total sincerity that "God has done great things for me!" It was an honor to be used by Him in such a manner. But she was not rejoicing alone. Mary was with Elizabeth, and together, they rejoiced regarding the life in her womb and the coming of the long-promised Savior!

So, Mary's response to the angel's extraordinary message was first *confusion*, followed by *obedience*, and then *joy*! To us, her response is both inspiring and disconcerting...especially if we want to model her unwavering faith, regardless of the consequences.

Learning from Mary

The Importance of Obedience

The first principle we take from Mary's life is simple to understand but not easy to do. Like Mary, we too are to trust God and His plans, even when that puts us outside of our comfort zones (notice I said "when" not "if"). Obedience should be our default response to God. But that's often easier said than done. Yet, as we learn from Mary's example, by obeying God, He can use us in extraordinary ways!

We also observed that Mary was able to rejoice amid her challenging circumstances because she was in the center of God's will. Even though she was part of a plan that seemed crazy—humanly speaking—she was to play a central role in the most important historical event of all time! She trusted God beyond her fear and, as such, He used her powerfully to accomplish His purposes and bless the world. Along the way, Mary was greatly blessed too.

From personal experience, I can also affirm that peace and joy can be found in the middle of swirling circumstances, as long as you remain in the center of God's will.

Lisa and I had been married for ten years, with two young sons. I was a reasonably successful businessman, and we had a comfortable life. But one day, we both sensed the Lord moving. He was nudging us into a season of change. God was calling us into full-time vocational ministry.

This was such a big change in direction that we could hardly believe it. As Lisa observed, "I married a businessman, not a pastor." As for me, vocational ministry was so foreign that I would later remark, "I thought I had a greater chance of being dead in five years than being a pastor."

Our friends and family thought we were crazy. They didn't understand why we would trade our comfortable lifestyle for ministry. But Lisa and I knew this was God's will for us, and we would obey His call.

I quit my job. We sold our house. We moved to Dallas and got the kids enrolled in school, just as I was accepted to Dallas Theological Seminary. And we couldn't imagine doing anything else.

It was, indeed, a huge change, and our friends and family were still quietly questioning our decision. But we felt an abiding sense of peace that could come only from God. Our world might be a hurricane, but God had us right in the calm eye of the storm. We learned that there's no better place to be than in the center of God's will, regardless of what's swirling around you!

The Futility of Disobedience

What if Mary had rejected God's will for her life? What if obedience was replaced with rebellion? Would she have been able to thwart God's plans? No. God's purposes were going to be accomplished regardless but, perhaps, not through Mary.

To put a point on the matter, you are either for God or against Him. There is no middle ground. We can either (1) obey God and be part of His plans, or (2) go our own way and stand against Him, thinking we know better. However, experience will eventually confirm that opposing God is not really a wise option.

Like many families, we long ago adopted the motto, "As for me and my household, we will serve the LORD!" We have come to trust that God's got this (whatever "this" is at the time), as our all-knowing, loving Creator. And He poignantly reminds us of His superiority, and ability to see beyond our limitations, in Isaiah 55:8-9 (ESV):

> "For my thoughts are not your thoughts, neither are your ways my ways," declares the LORD. "For as the heavens are higher than the earth, so are my ways higher than your ways and my thoughts than your thoughts."

If we choose to obey God—even when it makes no sense—then we can be used by Him in extraordinary ways, blessing others as we too are blessed. And joy will surely follow!

What is God asking you to do that's got you feeling uncomfortable? Maybe it's something that you've been avoiding. Remember, when ordinary people trust God, extraordinary things happen! Will you obey?

Celebrating the Arrival

Mary rejoiced with Elizabeth, as they anticipated the arrival of the promised Messiah. And Christmas is a perfect time for us to rejoice too. It's a time to celebrate the arrival of God's Son, who walked alongside people like you and me... and to expectantly await His earthly return!

Here are a few suggestions to help you get into the Christmas spirit, which do not involve shopping or spending money:

- Celebrate the best Gift ever given, who walked among us and offered the only way to escape eternal hopelessness and embrace unending joy.
- Recount your personal testimony of God's faithfulness, just as Mary did.
- Joyously anticipate all that God will do when His Son returns. Live like He's coming tomorrow while recognizing that it could be another thousand years.
- Demonstrate love for one another through various acts of kindness, mimicking the example of our Heavenly Father and the loving provision of His Son.

- Share the Good News of Jesus Christ[9] with friends and family members who don't understand the true meaning of Christmas. Give them a reason to really celebrate!

As we enter the Christmas Season—a time of parties, families, and presents—let me encourage you to resist the temptation to get swept up in the phony hoopla. Instead, remain firmly focused on the true "Reason for the Season," and the authentic joy that He brings!

Father in heaven, may I—like Mary—respond to your perfect will with obedience. And may I embrace the joy and wonder of your Son's arrival during this Christmas Season. For I pray these things in the matchless name of Jesus. Amen.

Personal Study: Going Deeper

Warm-up: What are you most thankful for regarding Christ's birth 2,000 years ago?

Scripture Reading: Luke 1:26-49

If you were Mary, how would you have responded, given the ramifications indicated in Luke 1:38?

- How much must you trust God in order to respond the way Mary did?
- Have you ever been asked by God to trust Him in a significant way? Did you trust Him or choose your own way instead? What are your thoughts on that decision today?

Many Jews of Mary's time longed for the Messiah. Their expected Savior was a Warrior-King who would crush the Romans. How surprised do you think they were to find out that the Son of God took both the humblest form (a baby) and was born into the humblest of circumstances?

- What does it mean to you that Immanuel ("God with us") entered the world as a baby in a manger?
- What does this tell us about God?
- Why should this be a source of great rejoicing for us, as children of God?

What are some of your favorite ways to share the joy of the Christmas Season with others?

3

Joseph's Response: Courage

Matthew 1:18-25

When was the last time that you watched a football game, and when they turned the TV camera on a star athlete, he said, "Hi, Dad"? Never! The fact is, he said "Hi, Mom!" like everyone else.

And who took that million-dollar athlete outside when he was a boy and taught him how to catch, throw, or hit the ball? Most times it was his father, or a man who assumed the role of a father figure. But who got recognized years later? Typically not that man.

Everyone knows that a mother is priceless in the life of a child. A mother nurtures, loves, and serves with little thought for herself. Being a mother is a highly valued role, and we see that in the life of Mary. Gabriel called Mary "highly favored by God," as the future mother of the Messiah. Elizabeth said that she was "blessed among women."

And Mary herself praised God because all generations would call her blessed.

But what about Joseph? Was he to be blessed among men for generations to come because of his role as Jesus' earthly father? Would history remember Joseph as fondly as Mary? The simple answer is no. None of the positive things linked to Mary are repeated in the Bible regarding Joseph.

In fact, the Scriptures do not record a single word uttered by Joseph. Perhaps he was a man of few words. Perhaps he didn't speak with great eloquence. But does that make Joseph an unimportant figure in the Messiah's birth and developmental years—as the one who had a hand in training up Jesus, providing for Him, and equipping Him with a trade? The answer is an emphatic no!

> Scripture does not record a single word uttered by Joseph.

However, what the Bible does record are Joseph's actions. And his actions speak louder than words ever could. With no promises of grand blessing, Joseph was greatly, but quietly, used by God to fulfill His purposes and bring about the arrival of the extraordinary Jesus.

Before we jump to the Scriptures, it's important to note that the historical, scriptural, and cultural contexts impacting Joseph's story are like those mentioned as part of Mary's. The Jews were expecting the Messiah to arrive at any time. He would assume the throne of David, His ancestor. There was strong dissatisfaction with the political situation. And godly family life did not allow for pregnancy outside of wedlock.

The Setting: A Dilemma Unfolds

Matthew's Gospel begins with a genealogy of the Messiah in order to establish His ancestral line from Abraham through King David.[10] Joseph is included in this list, as an often-cited descendant of David. Mary's lineage is not revealed in Scripture. This makes Joseph an important part of the messianic prophecies' fulfillment.

Once Jesus is firmly rooted in the redemptive history of Israel, Matthew provides some details surrounding His upcoming birth. Here we first encounter Joseph and his dilemma. Beginning in Matthew 1:18:

> This is how the birth of Jesus the Messiah came about: His mother Mary was pledged to be married [*NASB: had been betrothed*] to Joseph, but before they came together, she was found to be pregnant through the Holy Spirit.

A woman was considered of marriageable age once she had passed through puberty, while a man had to be established and able to support a family. This meant that Joseph was likely twice Mary's age. While Joseph did not live to see Jesus' messianic ministry, Mary was alive to see it, even witnessing His crucifixion and Pentecost.[11]

In keeping with the stipulations of betrothal, Mary and Joseph had not yet had intimate relations, which were out-of-bounds until they were formally married. According to the Law, this binding agreement could only be severed by divorce or death.

So, what was Joseph's dilemma? During the betrothal period, Mary was "found to be with child." In other words, Mary was pregnant before she and Joseph had consummated their marriage. Although Matthew added a bit of commentary explaining that this was done "through the Holy Spirit," how could Joseph have known? Given his—and our—understanding of marriage and children, Joseph surmised Mary had been unfaithful. He had a difficult dilemma on his hands.

Joseph's Plan

Joseph likely felt angry and betrayed upon learning about Mary's pregnancy. I'm sure he was heartbroken by the whole thing. But he still cared deeply for her. How to respond? We pick up the story in Matthew 1:19:

> Because Joseph her husband was a righteous man and did not want to expose her to public disgrace, he had in mind to divorce her quietly.

Joseph had a plan. The way he was going to handle his dilemma was by divorcing Mary. Recall that there were only two ways to end a betrothal: divorce or death. But let's not gloss over the fact that death was a viable option, should Joseph have made it one. As a betrothed couple, Mary and Joseph were legally bound to one another. As such, he could bring charges of adultery against her. And, although rarely employed by this time, the Law prescribed stoning as the penalty.

Yet, Joseph was not only a righteous man, but also a compassionate man. He planned to pursue a quiet divorce, in order to minimize the public humiliation of Mary and her family. Even when confronted with unspeakable heartbreak, Joseph responded with great compassion.

The Angel's Message

As Joseph finalized his plan that night and somehow fell asleep, an extraordinary encounter took place—in the form of a dream—which caused him to rethink his decision. Picking up in Matthew 1:20-23:

> But after he [*Joseph*] had considered this, an angel of the Lord appeared to him in a dream and said, "Joseph son of David, do not be afraid to take Mary home as your wife, because what is conceived in her is from the Holy Spirit. She will give birth to a son, and you are to give him the name Jesus, because he will save his people from

their sins." All this took place to fulfill what the Lord had said through the prophet: "The virgin will be with child and will give birth to a son, and they will call him Immanuel"—which means, "God with us."

Joseph, like Mary, received an angelic visitor. But unlike Mary's encounter, Joseph's angel was not named. The angel's message was simple: "do not be afraid." He was to suppress this very natural response to his situation and instead take action. Joseph was to take the next step in his relationship with Mary—to take her home as his wife—even though she was pregnant (and not by him).

Let's not miss this important insight. To *not* allow fear to keep you from doing what needs to be done is the definition of courage! So the angel's exhortation to Joseph was to put aside his fear and act courageously. He must do the right thing despite the expected consequences.

> Courage is about doing what must be done in spite of fear's presence.

Yet, the angel gave Joseph more than a simple command. He provided God's perspective on the situation, which was intended to help lessen Joseph's concern. Joseph learned Mary had conceived in a most miraculous way. The Baby within her womb was from the Holy Spirit and did not represent unfaithfulness on Mary's part. And this was not just any baby but *the* Baby, who would be called Jesus and save people from their sins. Joseph undoubtedly knew the messianic prophecies. Every good Jew did. Thus, he understood the angel could only be describing the arrival of the promised Messiah.

Joseph's Response: Courage

Joseph awoke from his dream, knowing that he was to scrap his divorce plans and move forward with Mary. But in the light of day, did he follow through or run? The answer is found in Matthew 1:24-25.

> When Joseph woke up, he did what the angel of the Lord had commanded him and took Mary home as his wife. But he had no union with her until she gave birth to a son. And he gave him the name Jesus.

Joseph responded with courage, putting his fear aside and taking Mary into his home. Undoubtedly, most things happened that had caused Joseph to fear in the first place. People questioned his character. They gossiped about the scandal of it all. The newlyweds were ostracized and laughed at. They lost friends. But Joseph courageously moved forward. He obediently did all that God had asked. And he did not allow his fears to get the better of him.

It's worth noting that Joseph was not only courageously obedient to God, but also exhibited the noteworthy trait of self-control. We are told that he brought Mary into his house but did not consummate the marriage until after she gave birth months later. Joseph may have been an ordinary man but, in my book, he exhibited extraordinary character, making him a noteworthy husband and father.

Summarizing Joseph's story: He faced a dilemma and developed a plan to deal with it. But an angel of the Lord revealed the truth to him in a dream. Joseph then exhibited exceptional courage and embraced God's plan over his own, despite the expected negative consequences. He did his part to help bring about the arrival of the Extraordinary. He was greatly, but quietly, used by God to fulfill His purposes.

Learning from Joseph

Like most of us, Joseph was just an ordinary guy. He grew up in an unremarkable town, loved God, got a job as a carpenter, and desired to start a family. He probably even got into a bit of mischief with his buddies when he was a teenager. But all of this is humble stuff, not the makings of a blockbuster Hollywood movie.

Yet because of Joseph's courageous obedience, God used him as an important part of His plan—to bring His only Son into the world.

The Importance of Trusting God

Put yourself in Joseph's sandals. Would you have responded to his dilemma in the same way that he did, with selfless courage? That's a tough question to answer, especially if your trust in God is wavering. Joseph did not do what he did because of his self-confidence or strength of character alone. He changed direction because he trusted God, the Rock of Ages and ultimate Promise Keeper. Joseph knew God loved him and had his back, which resulted in a trust that overpowered his very real fear.

So, is your faith strong enough to trust God not only with the little details of your life but also with the big, life-altering decisions? Think back on the many ways God has proven Himself faithful in your life. When fear and doubt creep in, recall these things as a reminder that God is trustworthy and will show up for you.

Our Good Ideas Are Not Always Right

Initially, Joseph concluded he had no choice but to divorce Mary. It seemed like a *good thing* to do. However, when he looked at it from God's perspective, he understood it was not the *right thing* to do.

We too, need to invite God to interact with our decisions before we act on them. As it says in Proverbs 16:3, "Commit to the LORD whatever you do, and your plans will succeed."

> I had a seminary professor, Dr. Howard Hendricks (everyone called him "Prof"), who shared a very practical way that he would go about making important decisions. He would begin by praying for a clear sense of God's leading.

Then he would evaluate all the information that he had available, "using the brain that God gave me." He would seek input from trusted advisors, as needed. Then he would finalize what he intended to do.

Before taking action, Prof would sleep on it. As he went to bed, he would pray, "Lord, I've done all that I know to do. If this is not your will, then please make it apparent to me." If, in the morning, he had a sense of peace about the decision, he would move forward.

Just as Dr. Hendricks slept on his decisions before taking action, Joseph developed his plan to divorce Mary, then slept on it. Because God had a chance to interact with his plans, Joseph could make a course correction and do the right thing.

So, like Joseph, our "good ideas" are not always right from God's perspective. We too, need to give Him a chance to interact with our decisions.

Dealing with Disappointment

From Joseph's experience, we also learn that understanding God's perspective can help heal our disappointments and heartbreaks. There is little doubt that Joseph was devastated by what he perceived as a serious violation of the vows he and Mary made to one another. However, when God revealed His perspective—that is, the correct perspective—on Mary's pregnancy, Joseph's outlook changed. He was no longer a man betrayed. He was now a man marrying the woman he loved and also the future earthly father of the promised Messiah!

On a certain level, we can all relate to Joseph's situation. How many times have we felt disappointed or even heartbroken by an unforeseen set of circumstances, not of our own making? But by understanding God's perspective—and seeing the true picture—it is possible to turn heartbreak into healing and even delight.

So, when you're in the middle of something difficult, take a moment to step back from your immediate circumstances and see the big picture. What might God be doing? What is it that God wants me to learn from this? Is there something I'm missing? Does His Word have anything to say about it? Does any of this help to reshape my understanding?

As part of God's family, we must not forget that no matter what happens here on earth, we win in the end! We will spend eternity in our Savior's presence, apart from any hint of discouragement, depression, disease, or death. For we have a hope that transcends our current circumstances!

An Everyday Courage

Joseph's example clearly teaches us something about courage, which is doing the right thing in spite of fear's presence. From our quick tour through Scripture, we saw Joseph was:

1. *A righteous man*...who desired to live a life that honored God.

2. *A trusting man*...who believed God's way was the best way.

3. *A courageous man*...who took action in obedience to God despite his fears.

Fear often causes us to do the wrong thing or, perhaps more often, avoid doing anything at all. Paraphrasing philosopher Edmund Burke, "The only thing necessary for the triumph of evil is for good men to do nothing." To overcome this fear, we need to believe in our hearts that obedience to God's plan is the right course of action, regardless of the consequences. And then take action. That is courage.

All noteworthy men and women of God have had to act courageously at one time or another. Since God's ways are not our ways and His thoughts are not our thoughts, God will eventually ask everyone who desires to be used by Him to do something that is counterintuitive, violating conventional wisdom. And that's where courage comes in.

Remember Joshua? He was asked to march around the city of Jericho and make a lot of noise for seven days. How's that for a sound military strategy? He probably looked like a total fool. But he trusted God more than he feared for his own reputation, and the city walls came tumbling down.

Perhaps God is asking you to do something that's got you feeling uneasy. The first step is to identify it. Maybe He's asking you to do something like: (1) turn down a promotion, (2) pursue a new friendship with a person who seems unapproachable, (3) start a new ministry endeavor, or (4) give your spouse a second chance. There are a thousand other things that can fit on this list. So, what's yours? Next, pray about it and ask God to show you the way. Finally, find inspiration in Joseph's example and courageously respond to God's leading in obedience!

Remember, the amazing arrival of our extraordinary Savior was made possible—at least in part—by the faith and courage of an ordinary man named Joseph, who trusted God more than his own fears.

Beloved Father, may I—like Joseph—confront my fears with courage and a commitment to action. And, as you call me to do difficult things, may I trust that you have my best interests at heart, as my good Father. For I pray these things in your Son's powerful name. Amen.

Personal Study: Going Deeper

Warm-up: How have you demonstrated courage in the past? What circumstances were present that required you to act courageously?

Scripture Reading: Matthew 1:18-25

How would you feel knowing that your wife-to-be was pregnant, and you were not the father? In Joseph's case, how hard might it be not to resent God?

How much courage does it take to respond to this situation as Joseph did? What are some of the possible ramifications of his decision (related to work, family, friends, his synagogue, etc.)?

- Have you ever been asked by God to trust Him this much?
- Did you trust Him or choose an easier path?
- If you chose the easier path, what did that experience teach you?

Why does it take courage to follow God faithfully?

How important a role do you think Joseph played in the birth and upbringing of the Christ-Child?

What are some of the key lessons you've learned from studying Joseph? How will they impact the way you live out your faith in Christ?

PART II

THE ARRIVAL

4

God's Response: Love

Luke 2:1-7

A young father sat near the Christmas tree on Christmas morning with his wife and daughter. After the little girl had finished opening all of her presents, she ran to her bedroom and brought back a present for her daddy. She was very proud of this present because she had decided on the gift herself—without help from Mommy—and wrapped it with all the skill her four-year-old hands could muster.

The little girl's mother looked at the package and then her husband, and shrugged. She had no idea what the small box contained.

The young father was excited. This was the first year his daughter had taken the initiative to give him a gift. What would it contain? "What would my little girl give me as a demonstration of her love for me?" he wondered. Although the package wasn't all that big and impressive, he still eyed it expectantly.

When the young man opened the box, he saw nothing in it. He was disappointed! Is this all he meant to his little girl? He worked so hard to provide for her! He even swallowed his pride and dressed up for her silly little tea parties! And what did she give him? Not even a picture scribbled in a coloring book at preschool!

Disappointment written on his face, the father looked at his little girl and said, "You can't give an empty box as a Christmas present. It has to have something in it. You've really hurt your daddy's feelings!"

His daughter began to cry—a whimper at first—but then she began sobbing. Through the tears, she pleaded, "Daddy, the box is full. It's full of kisses for you. I put every one of them in there myself!"[12]

Needless to say, the father felt like a heel. His daughter gave him the best present ever—a true token of her love for him—and he missed it!

It is so easy to look past the most precious gifts when we're busy looking for something else. That's how most people viewed the birth of Christ. It was not at all what they were expecting. It was just too ordinary. Yet, the birth of Immanuel represented a "box full of kisses" from God! Jesus' truly extraordinary arrival was overlooked. From humble and unassuming origins came the greatest Gift ever given...or received.

Historical Context

The Gospel writer, Luke, was a physician trained to be both observant and precise in the recording of details. His telling of Jesus' birth was no exception. He began by establishing the historical context in Luke 2:1-3.

> In those days [*which ties the following event to John the Baptist's birth in Luke 1*] Caesar Augustus issued a decree that a census should be taken of the entire Roman world. (This was the first census that took place while Quirinius was governor of Syria.) And everyone went to his own town to register.

Just before Jesus' arrival, Caesar Augustus issued a decree that required a census to be taken of "all the inhabited earth" (NASB), which is a more literal rendering of the Greek text. Augustus was the most powerful man in the world. He ruled Rome from 27 BC to AD 14, some forty-one years. Frankly, there wasn't much worth having that was not already part of Rome, which caused Luke to describe the Roman Empire as "all the inhabited earth."

Not only was Augustus the first emperor of Rome, but likely the best. He expanded its boundaries significantly and governed during a period of unprecedented peace and prosperity. It was said that he "came to a Rome made of bricks and left it a city of marble."[13] So, no one—no person, no country—could stand against Augustus' wishes without incurring the wrath of the most powerful man on earth!

Luke then transitioned in the telling of his story from Caesar and a census of the Roman world to the province of Syria, which included the land of Israel. Since no Jew had a choice as to whether they took part in the census, everyone went to their ancestral hometown at the appointed time. After arriving, each person registered with the authorities to pay taxes. In other places throughout the Roman Empire, the citizens also registered for military service. But not the Jews. They were legally exempt from serving because it required both work on the Sabbath and participation in emperor worship, violating Jewish Law. The pain of their service was considered greater than the benefit.

All of this detail begs the question: Why did Luke choose to give us a history lesson as he prepared to tell the story of Jesus' birth? Think of it this way. Secular history teaches that emperors, kings, and presidents—powerful political leaders—are the ones who shape the world. And at the time of Jesus' birth, it was Caesar Augustus who had the power. But Luke wants us to understand that it was God who was really in control of the situation. In fact, He was all-powerful and remains so!

> Augustus may have been powerful, but he unknowingly acted as an agent of God, doing His will.

So, Augustus was an agent of God, doing His will. Even though it was the emperor's decree that placed Mary and Joseph in Bethlehem for the Messiah's arrival, God was pulling the strings to ensure that they were in the right place at the right time to fulfill the prophecies. So, even the mighty Caesar had to conform to God's wishes!

Just as God Planned

Next, Luke moved from the province of Syria to the town of David and a young couple who were about to have a baby. Continuing with Luke 2:4-6:

> So Joseph also went up from the town of Nazareth in Galilee to Judea, to Bethlehem the town of David, because he belonged to the house and line of [*King*] David. He went there to register with Mary, who was pledged to be married to him and was expecting a child. While they were there, the time came for the baby to be born.

Joseph was required to travel from his residence in Nazareth to his ancestral hometown in Bethlehem for the census, a journey of some 90 miles[14] or four to five days. Joseph belonged to the lineage of King David—who ruled Israel a thousand years earlier—and was from Bethlehem. Mary joined Joseph on the journey. They were betrothed, yet Mary was pregnant.

While in Bethlehem registering for the census, the time came for Mary's Baby to be born. Don't neglect the tension that must have been present in the lives of Mary and Joseph. Although pledged to one another, they had not finalized their marriage—and Mary was expecting. From an outsider's point of view, this was a big problem!

Yet, Mary and Joseph knew the backstory, because an angel of God paid each of them a visit and explained the miraculous nature of the Baby's conception. We too, understand that there was nothing inappropriate going on between Mary and Joseph because we have the benefit of the New Testament. The Baby was God's Son, conceived by the Holy Spirit.

But what about the people who were contemporaries of Mary and Joseph, living before the New Testament was written? Would they have been able to discern the truth about her pregnancy? Possibly. But it would have required some effort on their part. The Hebrew Scriptures, written centuries before Jesus' birth, would have been an excellent place to start. Consider just these few representative verses:

Micah 5:2: The Messiah was to be born in Bethlehem.

Isaiah 7:14: The Messiah was to be born of a woman, a virgin.

Isaiah 9:6-7: The Messiah was to come from the line of David.

Even in those humble and hectic circumstances, the hand of God was visible to those who were willing to look. In fact, God set up His Son's arrival exactly as planned, in fulfillment of prophecy.

Finally! The Messiah Is Born

In one short verse, Luke described Jesus' birth. It's almost anticlimactic. Concluding the story in Luke 2:7:

> And she [Mary] gave birth to her firstborn, a son. She wrapped him in cloths and placed him in a manger, because there was no room for them in the inn.

Jesus' birth is described in simple, unadorned terms. It is relatively humble prose for the arrival of the greatest Gift ever given. But much is communicated in these few words.

First, Jesus was described as Mary's firstborn, which implied that she would eventually have other children. Interestingly, the Bible reports that Mary had four other sons (James, Joseph, Simon, Judas) and multiple daughters.[15] It also supported Jesus' eligibility to inherit David's throne as the firstborn son of a Davidic family, traced through Joseph (Jesus' legal, earthly father).

Next, we learn that the Baby Jesus was wrapped in strips of cloth and placed in a manger. His first outfit was not a cute onesie but scraps of cloth, wrapped tightly around His tiny body to keep Him warm and—so they believed—to ensure that His limbs would grow straight. But before being wrapped, Jesus' umbilical cord was cut and tied, and He was washed. Then He was rubbed with salt and oil and wrapped, keeping with the practices of the day.

The Messiah was then placed in a manger used for feeding animals. He was not born in a place intended for human habitation, but a stable fit for livestock. Church history further reveals that this stable was in a cave. Frankly, you can't get any further from palaces and kingly accouterments than caves, feeding troughs, and scraps of cloth. But then again, this extraordinary Savior didn't come primarily for the elites, but for the ordinary, overlooked people like you and me.

No Room at the Inn

Luke concluded by providing the reason for the Messiah's stable birth. With all the people traveling to Bethlehem for the census, the town was bursting at the seams with visitors who needed a place to stay. And so, "There was no room for them in the inn."

In those days, inns were nothing like the hotels of today, but more like youth hostels, with a large common room shared by the guests. Hay was thrown on the floor to provide some comfort as they lay down. It wasn't much. But an inn likely smelled better than a stable, was warmer, and kept the weather off your back.

Compared to Mary and Joseph's meager shelter, the inn was a 5-star hotel...which reminds me of a story.

A weary traveler came into a hotel and asked for a room. The manager told him they were fully booked and no rooms were available.

The man said, "Now be honest with me. If the President of the United States walked through that door just now and requested a room, would you have a place for him to stay?"

The manager replied, "Well, if the President needed a room, we'd find one for him."

The traveler said, "That's great. I know for a fact that he's not coming, so I'll take his room."[16]

Perhaps if Mary and Joseph were more influential people, there would have been a room for them, too. But they were ordinary people—peasants, carpenters, common laborers. So, they got no special favors and had no special place to stay...certainly no place worthy of a King!

Learning from the Precious Gift's Arrival

Let's explore some ways to apply the amazing nature of Jesus' birth to our lives.

Like You and Me but...

Mary gave birth to her Baby and cared for Him, like any ordinary newborn. Thus, God's Son entered the world in the same way as you and me. He was wrapped in cloth for warmth and a sense of security, just as we were.

Jesus could have entered the world in an impressive manner, perhaps floating down from the sky as a King with a lightning-bolt sword in His hand. But that wasn't part of the master plan. Rather, He was born in the customary way, taking the form of a small, helpless baby. Thus, we can identify with Jesus. And He can identify with us.

Take a moment and let that amazing truth sink in—then turn it on its head. On the one hand, being human, aspects of Jesus' life were so ordinary that we share them in common—we can relate. On the other hand, being God, He is so extraordinary as to be unfathomable.

The Son is now and will forever be both fully God and fully Human. Exactly how that works itself out is a mystery, but it is an essential truth of the Christian faith. And it's on display in the birth of this most precious little Boy.

Messy Birth, Messy World

Next, consider the unsanitary conditions in which Mary gave birth, as the couple carefully maneuvered around animals and their droppings. Can you imagine going through the pains of labor, and then placing the newborn Jesus in a feeding trough, infused with the smell of feed and streaked with animal saliva? That paints a picture of messy, humble beginnings.

> God sent His Son into a messy world to do a great work.

God sent His Son to a messy place, in a messy world, to do a great work. Although He deserved the introduction of a king, God had other plans. That's why Philippians 2:6-7 tells us that Jesus humbled Himself to take on the form of a man. He did this for the purpose of saving people from their sin. And our Savior Jesus is still at work in our sin-stained, messy world. This is the great work for which He came. He came for you and me!

No Room for a Savior?

Finally, we learned that there was no room for Joseph's little family at the inn. So, the Son of God arrived in a world that had no room for Him. That same world still had no room for a Savior years later, nailing Him to a cross. Even today, most people have no room for Jesus.

So, consider this: When Jesus was born, the world had no room for Him. But that doesn't have to include you. During this Christmas Season, will you make room for

Him, allowing Jesus to reclaim His position at the center of your celebration? Or will you—like the young father at the beginning of the chapter—overlook the precious Gift of God's Son, missing out on a box full of kisses sent to you from God?

Final Thought

The Savior of the world had very ordinary beginnings, but that was exactly the way God planned it. For Jesus was, is, and will forever be the single most extraordinary Person to walk the earth. His birth marked the promised new beginning for humankind. And that makes Jesus the single most precious Gift ever given...or received!

Father, thank you for sending your Son to earth, to take on flesh, and dwell among humankind. I praise you for loving me so much that you sent Him to die on a cross, that I might live. This was your perfect plan from the beginning, representing a new beginning for me and all who believe. Praise be to God! Amen.

Personal Study: Going Deeper

Warm-up: What thoughts and feelings first come to mind when you think of the birth of Baby Jesus? Why?

Scripture Reading: Luke 2:1-7

Looking at verses 1-4, in what ways can you see the hand of God behind the scenes, orchestrating events? Why do you think it was important that the Messiah's birth came about exactly as God planned it?

Meditate on verse 5. What is the primary source of tension it conveys?

- How do you think this tension might have affected the relationship between Mary and Joseph (from Mary's perspective, then from Joseph's perspective)?
- How might this tension have affected Mary and Joseph's relationships with other family members (such as Mary's mother and father)?
- How might this tension impact their relationships with their neighbors?
- Why do you think God chose to bring His Son into this kind of situation?

Referring to verses 6-7, list at least five things that can be learned about Jesus' birth.

- Why do you think God chose to bring His Son into the world in such a humble manner?
- In what ways do you identify with our Savior's birth, as described?
- What aspects of the Messiah's birth do you find most disconcerting? Why?
- What might you have thought and felt if you were there to see, touch, hear, and smell the Baby Jesus, knowing that He was God in flesh?

In what ways is God demonstrating His love for you through the sending of His Son?

Why is Jesus the best Gift ever given to you and all of humanity?

5

The Shepherd's Response: Belief

Luke 2:8-20

Christmas is BIG! It's the single biggest event of the year. It's associated with the biggest parties. The biggest expenses. And it creates the biggest expectations.

Christmas is so big that we often forget it's rooted in humble beginnings. It's easy to lose sight of the unpretentious people God used to bring about the birth of His Son and announce His arrival to the world.

I'm convinced that this Christmas Season we need "less big" and "more small." Less glitz and more substance. Why? God is especially fond of humble, upright people.

Think about Mary, the mother of Jesus. Mary was a simple girl from Nazareth. She was *not* a princess...*not* a priestess...*not* a star of stage and screen...*not* a fashion model.

How about Joseph, Jesus' earthly father? He was a carpenter of modest means. He was *not* wealthy...*not* well-connected...*not* powerful.

And who were the first people to receive an announcement of the Messiah's arrival? Let me tell you who they were *not*. The announcement did *not* go first to kings, Caesars, priests, popes, generals, or their armies. Instead, this most important message was initially shared with lowly shepherds, despised by people of position.

God loves humble and unassuming. God reveals Himself to humble and unassuming. God uses humble and unassuming people because they tend to understand their desperate need for a Savior.

The Backstory

Before continuing, let's review some important context. Jesus' birth is recorded in Luke 2:1-7, which contains some very particular details about the Messiah's arrival. This was intentionally done by Luke to prove that He came exactly as God planned, as foretold by the ancient prophets. But humanity's Savior was born in a very humble—even horrific—setting, in an animal pen, and laid in a feeding trough.

Why was He born in this way? Practically speaking, it was because there was no room for them at the inn. But it's much more than that. The Son of God came for all men, women, and children, from the lowest to the greatest. He was intended to be the perfect Gift for everyone!

If Jesus had been born in a palace, the poor would have had trouble identifying with Him. And as Dr. Darrel Bock states, "The Messiah's humble and common origins fit nicely with the task that he shall bear for all people, including especially the humble, hungry, and poor."[17]

Given God's love for the underdog, it's not surprising that immediately following the long-awaited birth, the news was first announced to some of the most humble and unassuming people around: shepherds.

The Shepherds Receive Good News

We pick up the story in Luke 2:8-9, right after Baby Jesus took His first breath and announced His arrival into the world with a newborn's cry.

> And there were shepherds living out in the fields nearby, keeping watch over their flocks at night. An angel of the Lord appeared to them, and the glory of the Lord shone around them, and they were terrified.

Have you ever noticed that everything scary happens when it's dark? The shepherds were initially afraid of the strange presence in their midst. In fact, the Greek text literally says that "they feared a great fear." So they were doubly fearful!

The shepherds were in the fields near Bethlehem, which put them some five miles south of Jerusalem. They were doing what all shepherds do at night: guarding their flocks. Raising sheep was big business so close to the temple. They had to keep the sacrifices plentiful for folks coming to worship. Thus, many shepherds must have been present that night.

In this culture, shepherds were considered low-class and lacked respect. They were societal outcasts. Since shepherds were constantly on the move, they were looked upon with suspicion, because they were unfamiliar to many of the people they encountered. They were often accused of being thieves. If something came up missing, it must have been those shepherds! In fact, they were often restricted from testifying in legal proceedings because their word wasn't considered trustworthy.

Shepherds were also considered religious outcasts. According to the Law, these men were unclean. Their line of work prevented them from participating in most of the feasts and holy days that made up the Jewish religious calendar. Someone had to watch the sheep while everyone else celebrated.

Finally, shepherds were, in essence, family outcasts. This was not a forty-hour-a-week job. Shepherds lived in the fields with their sheep. They didn't come home at night. Talk about 24/7! During the day, they led the sheep to grass and water and looked out for their well-being. At night, they slept in the sheep pen with the flock to guard against theft and wild animal attacks.

You get the picture. Being a shepherd was often lonely, boring, and tedious, but also potentially dangerous. These were humble men of humble means and low social standing.

Luke then reported that the shepherds encountered an unnamed angel. And "God's glory blazed among them" (MSG). This refers to the Shekinah Glory, indicating God's majestic presence. Needless to say, the whole thing had to be extremely frightening to the shepherds. It was like nothing else they'd ever seen!

Continuing with Luke 2:10-14:

> But the angel said to them, "Do not be afraid. I bring you good news of great joy that will be for all the people. Today in the town of David [*Bethlehem*] a Savior has been born to you; he is Christ the Lord. This will be a sign to you: You will find a baby wrapped in cloths and lying in a manger." Suddenly a great company of the heavenly host [MSG: *a huge angelic choir*] appeared with the angel, praising God and saying, "Glory to God in the highest, and on earth peace to men on whom his favor rests."

The angel brought an important message to the shepherds, which he termed "good news." They then learned the reason for the first Christmas. "A Savior has been born to you; he is the Messiah, the Lord." But why is Jesus called

"Savior"? Because He came to save people from having to pay the required penalty for their sins.

God's messenger then told the shepherds that this good news would result in great joy... for all humankind! Thus, at its core, Christmas is a joyous celebration of the good news!

> At its core, Christmas is a joyous celebration of the Good News!

The shepherds were to find the Savior in Bethlehem, just as the Scriptures foretold. This gave credibility to the angel's message. He also described the state in which the shepherds would find Baby Jesus: "wrapped in cloths and lying in a manger."

So, the shepherds received good news. The promised Messiah had arrived! And this news caused an angelic choir to assemble in celebration, singing God's praises!

But Why Shepherds?

Why did God choose to deliver this important good news first to shepherds? To many, it makes no sense.

When a child is born to a member of British royalty—like when Prince William and his wife Kate had a son (George)—they don't send a messenger down to the docks to break the news first to the longshoremen and the fishmongers. They don't issue personal invitations to the cab drivers of London.

They sent announcements to political leaders and foreign heads of state on gold-leaf stationery. And to the commoners, they post a sheet of paper outside of the castle.

The point is, you wouldn't expect an event like the birth of the King of kings and Lord of lords to be announced to the humblest people first but the most important. However, God chose not to go big first. As Max Lucado explains

The announcement went first to the shepherds. They didn't ask God if he was sure he knew what he was doing. Had the angel gone to the theologians, they would have first consulted their commentaries. Had he gone to the elite, they would have looked around to see if anyone was watching. Had he gone to the rich and successful, they would have first looked at their calendars to see if they had any conflicts.

So the message of the Messiah's arrival went first to the shepherds, men who didn't have a reputation to protect, an ax to grind or a ladder to climb. Men who didn't know enough to tell God that angels don't sing to sheep and that messiahs aren't found wrapped in rags and sleeping in a feeding trough.

To witness the Savior, you have to get on your knees. So, while the theologians were sleeping and the elite were dreaming and the successful were snoring, the meek were kneeling...they were kneeling in front of Jesus.[18]

The Shepherds Respond to the Good News

Picking up with Luke 2:15-16:

> When the angels had left them and gone into heaven, the shepherds said to one another, "Let's go to Bethlehem and see this thing that has happened, which the Lord has told us about." So they hurried off and found Mary and Joseph, and the baby, who was lying in the manger.

After the angel delivered his message, the shepherds got together and emphatically stated their desire to go and see what they had just heard about. We know this desire was strongly felt because the Greek text literally reads, "Indeed, let's go to Bethlehem!" In other words, the urge to go was so strong that they could think of doing nothing else!

Undergirding this desire to see the Baby, "which the Lord has told us about," was belief. They had a strong desire to "go" and "see" because they believed the Messiah had finally arrived, just as the Lord told them and just as the ancient prophets foretold.

The shepherds were not disappointed. When they arrived at the manger, something almost unimaginable took place. For the first time ever, they could see, hear, smell, and even touch the long-promised Baby, Jesus Messiah. They experienced God Himself, in a very tangible way. How amazing that must have been!

The Shepherds Share the Good News

After seeing the Babe for themselves, the shepherds could not contain their joy. Continuing with Luke 2:17-19:

> When they [*the shepherds*] had seen him [*the promised Messiah*], they spread the word concerning what had been told them about this child. And all who heard it were amazed at what the shepherds said to them. But Mary treasured up all these things and pondered them in her heart.

Once the shepherds experienced the newborn Messiah for themselves, they went out and shared the news with anyone who would listen. They were keenly aware that this most precious Gift was given to all people, so His arrival must not be kept quiet! Belief in the Savior's arrival—and the good news that it represented—resulted in a passion to share it with others.

The people were *amazed* by the shepherds' testimony. Yet, this single word doesn't quite capture the totality of the Greek word used by Luke. It is rooted in amazement and wonder but also encompasses reverence and adoration—the kind of worshipful response typically reserved for God. So, the hearers of the shepherds' testimony certainly understood the significance of the Baby's arrival.

Yet you might wonder why Luke inserted a sentence featuring Mary's restrained perspective amid the wonder and amazement of others. It almost seems like an aside that should be in parentheses. Although we can't be certain why it was included, we can certainly gain insight from it.

Mary's response to the good news—treasuring and pondering it, over time—serves as a contrasting response to those who were amazed in the moment. No doubt, Mary understood the significance of the Savior's arrival, but she was still trying to put together a more comprehensive understanding of all that was happening. If we place ourselves in Mary's shoes, as a young teenage mom, it's not a stretch to conclude that she was feeling a bit overwhelmed. She needed some time to get her head around it. Also, the inclusion of Mary's inner thoughts indicates she was likely a source for Luke's Gospel, adding credibility to his account of the birth.

Returning to the shepherds, their story ends in 2:20:

> The shepherds returned, glorifying and praising God for all the things they had heard and seen, which were just as they had been told.

That which the shepherds heard from the angel came to pass. They returned from the night's activities with their belief in God's Son firmly entrenched and even overflowing. This produced a profound sense of joy, driving them to worship God, glorifying and praising Him for His faithfulness in providing the promised Messiah.

Fast forward to today: A personal encounter with Jesus Christ should drive us to worship God too. And our Christmases should likewise be characterized by joy, awe, and wonder, as we celebrate the arrival of the ultimate Christmas Gift.

I know this sounds obvious, but it's worth repeating. Given the literal meaning of the word Christmas, it's difficult to celebrate it without Christ. To remove Him from Christmas is like planning a big birthday party for your best friend, then forgetting to invite the guest of honor.

Likewise, at Christmastime, we can go through all the decorating, buying presents, and preparing beautiful desserts, only to find out that we forgot to invite the birthday Boy—Jesus Christ—to His own birthday party!

> I heard of one family who tried to keep the focus squarely on Christ by putting an extra place setting at their table for Jesus during the Christmas Season. They took to calling Christmas, "Jesus' birthday party." When one of their daughters was asked if she got everything she wanted for Christmas, she answered by saying, "No. But then again, it's not my birthday."

Learning from the Shepherds

So let's summarize. God chose to celebrate the first Christmas with shepherds, who were humble, ordinary people. They were not at all like those one might expect, given the importance of the One arriving.

- Yet, God made sure it was the shepherds who first *heard* the good news.
- Then, those shepherds responded to the good news with *belief.*
- Finally, they *shared* the good news with others, praising and glorifying God.

Let's explore some important insights from the shepherds' story that can be applied to our own lives.

God Meets Us Where We Are

The shepherds weren't looking for answers to life's deeper meaning. They were just doing their job in the fields. At the appointed time, God's angel shared the good news with them. In choosing the shepherds, God showed us He was not interested in anyone's social status. In fact, He loves us all. He wants us all. And He meets us all exactly where we are. So, we are not directed to seek God on some high mountaintop or in a holy temple. No, God came to us as a Baby, called Immanuel. And that's the amazing thing about Christianity. God comes to us and meets us where we are!

God Calls Us to Respond to His Son

Once the shepherds heard the truth, they wanted to see Jesus personally. They showed us the proper response to hearing about Jesus by going directly to Him and meeting Him. Likewise, God's done all the work necessary to save us and even reached out to us, but we've still got to respond to the truth that He presents.

This principle is powerfully illustrated by a caring father at Christmastime.

Joshua loves to give presents to his children. And he has a real knack for knowing exactly what each child wants and needs. Joshua spends the entire year shopping, buying, hiding, and wrapping presents—which he also loves—because he's certain that what he's purchased will bring His children great joy!

When Christmas Eve comes and his loved ones are nestled snug in their beds, Joshua gets the presents out of hiding and neatly places them under the tree. He goes to bed satisfied that these gifts are just what his children need, gifts that will bring them joy and happiness. As Joshua closes his eyes, he knows that all the effort and sacrifice is worth it.

Finally, when the sun rises on Christmas morning, Joshua is up early. As his children come downstairs, they are greeted by a warm hug, a glowing fire, and a heartfelt "Merry Christmas" from their father.

This scene looks like a Norman Rockwell painting. It's absolutely perfect, except for one thing. Joshua's children simply refuse to open their presents.

His children look at the beautifully wrapped boxes with their names written on them, say "That's nice Dad," and go on like any other day. The TV comes on, the boys start wrestling, a mad dash is on for the last of the Captain Crunch, and the girls argue over who gets the shower first. Life goes on as normal. And everyone overlooks the perfect gifts sitting right under their noses![19]

Many of us are like these children. God has given us the perfect Gift in His Son—exactly what we need. We look at Him, say "that's nice," and move on to something else. But God desires for us to recognize His perfect Gift and respond to Him appropriately. He's selected this Gift for you, made sure it's exactly what you need, and presented it to you, saying, "Here you go, from Me to you, with love." But you've got to open it! God calls us to respond to His Son.

An Encounter with Jesus Is Meant to be Shared

What greater gift could God give us? What more is there that He could have offered? He didn't even withhold His own Son! And once the shepherds saw Jesus in person, they could not help themselves. They experienced an overflowing joy that could not be contained. They had to share what they had learned with others!

The same is true for us. Once we've met Jesus personally, we also experience an abounding joy. When we recognize all God has done for us through His Son, we understand what true love looks like. This drives us to share Jesus with other people in our lives. For love's sake, we must pass it on!

If you had the best gift in all the world to give away—a gift of infinite value that costs nothing to give; a gift that wouldn't run out but could be given to everyone—would you not be handing out that gift with abandon? Would people not start calling you Saint Nicholas?

Yet some people object: "I'm not an evangelist. I haven't been to seminary. I'm not rich or famous. No one will listen to me."

But it doesn't matter who you are or where you come from. God will use you if you'll let Him. Remember, He loves to use ordinary people from unassuming backgrounds!

God desires to use you in amazing ways, if you'll let Him.

Let's end with this: The Messiah's humble arrival was first announced to humble people who spread the good news to other ordinary people. God loves small and God loves humble. And He loves you so much that He sent you the perfect Gift. And that Gift is meant to be shared with others.

So, celebrate and share the good news of Jesus' arrival this Christmas Season! It's not meant to be kept a secret. And there really is no such thing as Christmas without Him!

Gracious heavenly Father, may we—like the shepherds—share our love of Jesus Messiah with others this Christmas Season. And may we experience afresh the wonder of your Son, Immanuel, as we celebrate His birth. For we pray these things in the name of our Lord and Savior. Amen.

Personal Study: Going Deeper

Warm-up: Why do you celebrate Christmas?

Scripture Reading: Luke 2:1-20

What do verses 10-11 tell us as to why the first Christmas was celebrated? Is this still the primary reason we should celebrate Christmas today?

- Do your reasons for celebrating Christmas match the reasons the shepherds celebrated the first Christmas? If not, how are they different?
- How can you better focus on the scriptural basis of Christmas this year?

When the shepherds learned the "good news," how did they respond to it in verses 15-16? In verses 17-18? In verse 20?

- How will these insights change the way you celebrate Christmas this year?
- Specifically, with whom are you going to share the good news of our Savior's coming (as the shepherds did in verse 17) this Christmas Season?

May your Christmas be filled with joy, awe, and wonder!

6

Interlude: Your Response

Sarah was doing some last-minute Christmas shopping at the mall. She was tired of fighting the crowds. She was tired of standing in lines. She was tired of weaving her way down long aisles looking for a gift that had sold out days before.

Her arms were loaded with bulky packages when the elevator door opened. It was full. The occupants on the elevator grudgingly tightened ranks to allow a small space for her and her purchases.

As the doors closed, Sarah blurted out, "Whoever is responsible for this whole Christmas thing ought to be punished severely!" A few others nodded their heads or grunted in agreement.

Then, from somewhere in the back of the elevator, came a single voice: "Don't worry. They've already crucified Him."[20]

And that's the point. Christmas is not about buying stuff and fighting crowds. It's not about trees or decorations, although these can be meaningful traditions. Christmas is about Christ. Did you ever wonder how we got the name *Christmas* for the event we celebrate on December 25? That day was originally called Christ's Mass, with *mass* being a Latin word meaning "the dismissal" or "the sending." So, the *mass of Christ*—or Christmas—is "the sending of Christ."

Thus, we celebrate Christmas to commemorate the sending of God's "anointed one" to earth. Or, from our point of view, we celebrate the arrival of this special Baby, named Jesus. But He was not only "God made flesh" and meant to walk the earth among us. He was ultimately sent by His Father to die on the cross for you and for me, to "save his people from their sins" (Matthew 1:21). Jesus' death for our lives.

That's why Jesus Christ is the only perfect Christmas Gift for every man, woman, and child. He meets us at our point of greatest need. Only He can fulfill the deepest desires of our hearts and grant eternal life, so that we don't have to live in fear of death!

> Only Jesus can fulfill the deepest desire of your heart.

Status Check

I don't know where you find yourself this Christmas Season. Perhaps you've never thought much about Jesus and you're considering Him for the first time.

Or perhaps you've been part of a church in the past, but life happened, and you got too busy to keep up with it.

Maybe you find yourself so down this Christmas Season that you don't know what to do. Regardless, you can't shake the feeling that something is missing; something is profoundly wrong.

How you answer this next question might help you better understand that feeling: Do you have a personal relationship with Jesus? To put it another way, have you trusted Jesus Christ as your Lord and Savior?

If your answer is "no" or "I'm not sure," then I've got something to share with you, which has the power to change your life. Found in the Bible, it contains both bad news, which has something to do with you and me, and good news, which has something to do with God.[21]

First, the BAD NEWS.

We are all sinners...that is, we've all missed the mark and fallen short of God's perfect standard. There are no exceptions. If you have a pulse, you've done things that you're not proud of and know are wrong.

As the Bible says in Romans 3:23,

For all have sinned and fall short of the glory of God.

Because of our sin, we're separated from God. In fact, because of our thoughts and actions, we've earned death [*that is, eternal separation from God*]. Many call this eternal separation "Hell." The Bible puts it simply in Romans 6:23:

The wages of sin is death.

Now, that's bad news. But God loves you too much to leave you stuck in your sin. Since there is no way for you to get to God on your own, the Bible says that He came to us through the sending of His Son, Jesus Christ. And, as we discussed earlier, that's the true meaning of Christmas!

So, now for the GOOD NEWS.

Jesus died for you! He sacrificed Himself on the cross to pay the penalty for your sin. That's why we call Him Savior. He saved us from having to pay the penalty for our own sin, which would have resulted in eternal separation from God.

This important truth is affirmed in the Bible, Romans 5:8 (NASB), which says

> God demonstrates His own love toward us, in that while we were still sinners, Christ died for us.

And you can be saved from your sin through faith in Jesus Christ, receiving the free gift of eternal life. That current separation between you and God can only be erased by faith in Jesus.

So, let me be clear. Faith in Jesus is the only solution to your sin problem. There's literally nothing you can do to be reconciled to God on your own. Being good won't do it. Giving money to your favorite charity won't do it. No good work you do is enough to pay the price for your sin. Only faith in Jesus will do.

Only Jesus—who lived a perfect, sinless life—is worthy of taking your place and making your sin payment. Ephesians 2:8-9 (NASB) puts it this way:

> For by grace [*undeserved favor*] you have been saved through faith [*in Jesus Christ*]; and that not of yourselves, it is the gift of God; not as a result of works, so that no one may boast.

To have *faith* means to *trust*. But what must you trust Christ for? You must depend on Him alone to pay the penalty for your sin, forgive you, and grant you eternal life.

So check this out.

When Jesus was born, they wrapped Him in cloths.

When Jesus died for you and me, they wrapped Him in cloths.

When Jesus was born, He was laid in a cave.

When Jesus died for you and me, He was laid in a cave.

When Jesus was born, there was no room for Him at the inn.

And now that Jesus has died for you, will you make room for Him? Or will you overlook this truly precious Gift? The choice is yours!

If you've just decided to trust Jesus, you're now part of God's family and He wants to hear from you. Take a moment to share your heart with Him by praying:

Dear God, I know that I'm a sinner. I know my sin deserves to be punished. I believe Jesus died for me and rose from the grave. I trust Him alone as my Savior. Thank you for the forgiveness and everlasting life I now have. In Your Son Jesus' name I pray. Amen.

You might find it difficult to comprehend the depth and breadth of God's love for you. So, I want to end with these encouraging words.

> God is crazy about you. If He had a refrigerator, your picture would be on it. If He had a wallet, your picture would be in it. Whenever you would talk, God would listen. And you might go days without thinking of Him, but there would never be a moment when He would not be thinking of you.[22]

PART III
AFTER THE ARRIVAL

7

Simeon's Response: Patience

Luke 2:22-35

The summer after I turned eight, I got it into my head that I NEEDED a dirt bike. My dad had a motorcycle, so I thought it was only fitting that I have one too. Specifically, I wanted—no NEEDED—a 1974 yellow Yamaha GT80 mini-bike.

Early in November, I was asked to put together my Christmas list. I took great care in preparing a special edition just for Grandma Dee. It was accompanied by a letter (and a Yamaha brochure), explaining my request. It said that, if she got me the mini-bike I so desperately wanted, she wouldn't have to get me a Christmas present for the next three years. How I picked three years I'll never know, but that seemed very logical to me as an eight-year-old.

A few days after mailing everything, I called my grandmother and asked, "Have you received my list?" "Yes," she replied. Then I swallowed hard and charged forward:

"Any chance of getting that mini-bike?" Her reply was encouraging: "I have little doubt that you'll be riding around on two wheels this Christmas morning."

GREAT! I was thrilled! Now it was a waiting game. But waiting for that promise to become reality seemed like it took forever. And in kid-time, it did. I knew I needed to be patient, but it was almost more than I could bear.

Finally, Christmas morning arrived. I was bouncing off the walls. I don't think I slept a wink. When my mom finally said it was OK to go downstairs, I thought my head would explode! The day I had patiently awaited had arrived!

I ran downstairs and saw the "two wheels" I'd be riding that very morning...a new bicycle.

The life lesson I learned as a young boy remains with me even today: Exhibiting patience can be challenging, but the ends typically justify the wait. And Simeon's story, found in Luke's Gospel, demonstrates this virtue to a much greater extent. He was an exceedingly patient man who was waiting on God to honor a promise made to him years earlier.

But unlike my Christmas gift, Simeon was in no way disappointed in the Gift God delivered to fulfill His promise. This ordinary man would have an extraordinary encounter with the Messiah, Baby Jesus, who was the One he had waited a lifetime to meet.

Setting the Stage for Simeon's Story

Let's begin with a quick review. We first explored Mary's story and the extraordinary way in which her Child was conceived by the Holy Spirit. Then we probed Joseph's encounter with an angel and his courageous response. Next, we investigated the advent of an extraordinary Baby, born into very ordinary circumstances. Finally, we examined the shepherds' story and how they responded to an extraordinary birth with faith.

Now, we turn to Simeon, picking up his story just weeks after Jesus' birth. Beginning with Luke 2:22-24:

> When the time of their purification according to the Law of Moses had been completed, Joseph and Mary took him [*Jesus*] to Jerusalem to present him to the Lord (as it is written in the Law of the Lord, "Every firstborn male is to be consecrated to the Lord"), and to offer a sacrifice in keeping with what is said in the Law of the Lord: "a pair of doves or two young pigeons."

The author placed Mary, Joseph, and Baby Jesus at the temple in Jerusalem. Although not obvious, two different things were going on. One involved Mary's purification, and the other involved Jesus' presentation and dedication.

First, Mary. According to the Law, women who gave birth were considered ceremonially unclean until they provided a purification offering at the temple, which was to take place forty days after delivery.[23] So, this scene must have occurred when Baby Jesus was around forty days old.

Luke then tells us that Mary's purification offering included "a pair of doves or two young pigeons." Thus, Mary and Joseph were pious people who observed the Law in obedience to God. But they were also people of humble means, as indicated by their offering of two birds (a lamb was required for those who could afford it). But how would this purification offering be made? Following accepted custom, Mary would have laid her hands on the birds. Then a priest would have sacrificed one bird as a sin offering and the other as a whole burnt offering.

Next, we turn our attention to Jesus. As parents, Mary and Joseph were also required by the Law to "consecrate" or "dedicate" Jesus—a firstborn son—to God.[24] Interestingly, all firstborn sons were to be set apart for the Lord's service. However, by this time, the Levites were tasked with serving God on behalf of all firstborn males. So, Jesus' parents paid a five-shekel fee at the temple to "redeem" Him from this service requirement.[25]

Waiting on a Promise

With the stage set, we're introduced to Simeon. Picking up with Luke 2:25-27:

> Now there was a man in Jerusalem called Simeon, who was righteous and devout. He was waiting for the consolation of Israel, and the Holy Spirit was upon him. It had been revealed to him by the Holy Spirit that he would not die before he had seen the Lord's Christ. Moved by the Spirit, he went into the temple courts.

Simeon is described as a godly man, both righteous and devout. He is not mentioned anywhere else in the Bible, so we don't know much about him. But what we do know is enough to establish him as a valuable role model.

Simeon looked forward to the arrival of the promised Christ, described as "the consolation of Israel." In this title for the Messiah, Simeon was looking towards the healing and restoration of Israel. The idea is found in Isaiah, where the Messiah is portrayed as a comforter who will save His people from their sin.[26] In short, Simeon was waiting for that which God had promised Israel long ago, with a great sense of excitement and expectancy!

Promise Fulfilled

Returning to Luke 2:27-29, God fulfills his promise to Simeon:

> When the parents [*Mary and Joseph*] brought in the child Jesus to do for him what the custom of the Law required, Simeon took him in his arms and praised God, saying: "Sovereign Lord, as you have promised, you now dismiss your servant in peace.

At the Holy Spirit's leading, Simeon went to the temple, where he encountered the promised Christ-Child. As he lovingly cradled the Babe in his arms, he praised God![27] In particular, Simeon was thankful for the Messiah's arrival and God's faithfulness. *Yahweh-Yireh*[28] had indeed provided a Savior, fulfilling His promise to Simeon, which served as the crowning moment of his life. And with that, Simeon was released to die in peace.

Evidently, Simeon was older and had been waiting to encounter the Messiah for quite some time. But he persevered over the years. Because of Simeon's great patience, he was rewarded with an extraordinary encounter, as he came face-to-face with "God made flesh."

> Today we find ourselves in a similar situation, as twenty-first century Christians. Like Simeon, we know Christ will come (in our case, come again). This was also promised to us by God generations ago.

How do you view the Messiah's imminent arrival? Like Simeon, do you wait with a sense of expectancy and excitement? Or is it a "ho-hum" kind of thing? Maybe you don't even think about it.

Imagine the emotional and theological richness that an appreciation for Christ's return could add to your Advent observance!

For Simeon's entire life, he held onto God's promise of a coming Deliverer. But, through the Holy Spirit who "was upon him," God specifically promised Simeon that he would see the Messiah during his lifetime. Thus, Simeon's expectation was not based on wishful thinking, but backed by the full faith and credit of God Himself!

Furthermore, Simeon responded to the leading of the Spirit on a moment-by-moment basis. He clearly had a rich and intimate relationship with God. When the Spirit told Simeon to go, he got up and went to the temple! Think of it: he had to arrive on the right day, at the right time, and in the right place, in order to encounter the long-awaited Christ! The result? Simeon moved when directed, and was rewarded for both his patience and obedience.

Salvation Arrives

Continuing with Luke 2:30-32, Simeon explained how God had fulfilled His promise.

> For my eyes have seen your salvation [*referring to the Christ*], which you have prepared in the sight of all people, a light for revelation to the Gentiles and for glory to your people Israel.

Simeon affirmed that he had seen the source of God's promised salvation—the Messiah—with his own eyes (and even held Him in his arms). This is important for at least two reasons. First, "God in the flesh" had arrived and, for the first time ever, the Lord was both seeable and touchable! Second, Jesus was indeed the long-promised source of salvation, as His name conveyed: God saves.

Simeon continued, articulating the purpose of the Messiah's coming: "I have seen your salvation, which you have prepared for all people" (NLT). In other words, reconciliation to God, through faith in Jesus Christ, is now available to everyone! This speaks to the universal nature of God's redemptive work. Jesus Christ did not come for the Jews alone, but for all people. The truth about God, as revealed through His Son, Jesus, is available to everyone! As for the Jews who already knew about this "Light," who have patiently awaited His arrival, the Messiah is their pride and joy...bringing glory and honor to the people of Israel!

Jesus' Parents Respond

Luke inserted a single sentence into his narrative, revealing Mary and Joseph's reaction to their encounter with Simeon, found in Luke 2:33.

> The child's father and mother marveled at what was said [*by Simeon*] about him [*Baby Jesus*].

When Mary and Joseph heard Simeon's prophecy, they "marveled" at it. To marvel is to be filled with surprise, wonder, and amazement. The fact that the little Baby, which Mary birthed, nursed, and comforted, would be the Savior of Israel and even all nations? That had to be mind-boggling!

Mary and Joseph certainly had some idea of what this special Baby represented. But as Dr. Darrel Bock observed: "The parent's response was natural since revelation about Jesus just kept coming."[29] They kept learning new things about their Baby, which caused them to wonder in amazement at all that Simeon told them. Likewise, the reality of our Savior's arrival ought to cause us to marvel too, as we contemplate His importance...not just to us, but to the entire world!

Opposition Will Emerge

Finally, Simeon ended his extraordinary encounter with an unsettling prophecy. Returning to Luke 2:34-35:

> Then Simeon blessed them and said to Mary, his mother: "This child is destined to cause the falling and rising of many in Israel, and to be a sign that will be spoken against, so that the thoughts of many hearts will be revealed. And a sword will pierce your own soul too."

Simeon's pronouncements took an ominous turn, from praise to warning. All men will not bow at the feet of the Messiah and opposition will emerge. As Dr. Bock again observes, "Simeon knows that although Jesus is God's hope, not everyone will respond positively to Him. The raising of this aspect of Jesus' fate is Luke's first indication that all will not go smoothly for God's anointed."[30]

We also learn that the Christ "is destined to cause the rising and falling of many." To the *humble*, Christ's coming is welcomed because they understand their need of a Savior. To the *haughty*, Jesus' coming is something to be resisted, because He represents judgement and their downfall.

Simeon continued, "the thoughts of many hearts will be revealed." So, one's true beliefs about God's Son will no longer be hidden. And everyone will fall into one of two groups. You will either be a friend of God, or His enemy.

The prophecy concluded with a heart-wrenching word of caution for Mary, linking her destiny to that of her Son and Savior, Jesus. "A sword will pierce your own soul too." This foreshadowed the fulfillment of Isaiah 53:5, as Jesus was physically "pierced" while on the cross.[31] But it more directly referred to the deep emotional pain that Mary would feel, as her Son was unjustly treated and killed. In fact, Mary would be present at Jesus' crucifixion and experience all the horrors firsthand,[32] in fulfillment of Simeon's temple prophecy.

So, the fact that many rose in opposition to our Savior implies opposition may eventually come for us too. Conflict inevitably arises between a world that uncompromisingly seeks to conform God's children to its image, while we seek to become more like Jesus, its polar opposite. Thus, we may

> Many rose in opposition to Jesus. They may eventually come for us too.

be required to be a sort of non-conformist or maverick—from the world's perspective—as we chart a course that remains true to God and His purposes. In short, we must be ready to think, act, and live differently than the world does. And that means that we are not precluded from experiencing the things our Savior did, including injustice, suffering, and even death.

How's that for Christmas cheer? But it's in the Bible. So we should not shy away from it as we survey the complete story of the most extraordinary Gift ever given, and His purpose in coming. If anything, keeping Jesus' eventual crucifixion in mind helps us to better appreciate His coming in the first place, and the priceless Gift He represents.

Learning from Simeon's Story

Simeon waited patiently on a promise made to him by God. And that promise was fulfilled through a divinely orchestrated encounter with the Christ-Child. So, given what we've learned, how should Simeon's example impact the way we live?

Be a Mover

When the Holy Spirit told Simeon it was time to move, he got up and went. Because of his sensitivity to the Spirit's leading, he saw the Messiah with his own eyes. He experienced a great blessing!

As believers, we too have the Spirit to lead us. Are you sensitive to His leading? Do you take time out of each day to seek the Lord's will for your life through the leading ministry of the Holy Spirit? If God wants to use you for His purposes, will you heed His call? If blessing comes your way, will you miss it?

So, be available to be used by God. Stand up and say, "Here I am Lord, use me." And when He tells you to move, move!

Share the Message

The Savior's arrival represented good news for Jews and Gentiles alike. Through the promised Messiah there is salvation—a Light in the darkness—representing the only genuine hope for humanity.

So, where would we be if someone had not shared the Good News with us? How can the people be saved if no one brings the Good News? As the Apostle Paul exhorted in Romans 10:13-15:

> For, "Everyone who calls on the name of the Lord will be saved." How, then, can they call on the one they have not believed in? And how can they believe in the one of whom they have not heard? And how can they hear without someone preaching to them? And how can they preach unless they are sent? As it is written, "How beautiful are the feet of those who bring good news!"

People are more open to hearing about Jesus at Christmas than most any other time of the year. So share the Gospel and be a blessing to others!

Experience the Marvel

Upon learning more of Jesus' purpose through the prophet Simeon, Mary and Joseph marveled. They were amazed!

Likewise, we too should marvel when experiencing the wonder of "God made flesh." It should never get old! Remember that because Almighty God—infinite, perfect, and complete—was willing to become one of us, a Savior entered the world who sought to rescue us from sin and death...which is surprising! Amazing! Wonderful! And should leave even the most hardened believers speechless.

Be a Maverick

Simeon revealed that the arrival of the promised Messiah would generate opposition, as the true nature of peoples' hearts was revealed. Thus, people would either be for Him or against Him.

As Jesus' disciples, we too may experience opposition if we live life in a manner that is pleasing to God. We will not always be popular. There will be pressure to conform to the world's standards. But we must stand firm in the face of opposition, just as our Savior did, making us a sort of maverick. But what does that look like?

The world: Hate those who hate you.
God's Word: Love your enemy.

The world: Whoever dies with the most toys wins.
God's Word: If you have two coats, give one to
    another in need.

The world: If my spouse doesn't meet my needs, I'll
    find someone who does.
God's Word: The two are one flesh, joined together
    by God.

The world: If you're good, let the whole world know.
God's Word: The meek shall inherit the earth.

These truths are revolutionary. Living them will make you a maverick. The world will view you as a threat who must be shut up and made to conform. But our Lord has promised to come again to separate the sheep from the goats.[33]

So, we must not be afraid to make the unpopular decisions, putting God first in our hearts, minds, and actions. As Jesus Himself said in Luke 12:51-53:

> Do you think I came to bring peace on earth? No, I tell you, but division [*dividing those who have a personal relationship with Jesus and those who have rejected Him*]. From now on there will be five in one family divided against each other, three against two and two against three. They will be divided, father against son and son against father, mother against daughter and daughter against mother, mother-in-law against daughter-in-law and daughter-in-law against mother-in-law.

The Singular Importance of the Son

A story is told of a man and his son, which should bring this idea home.

> Many years ago, a certain wealthy man shared a passion for art collecting with his son. They had priceless works of art adorning the walls of their family estate.

As winter approached, war engulfed the nation, and the young man left to serve his country. After only a few short months, his father received a telegram. His son had died.

Distraught and lonely, the old man faced the upcoming Christmas Season with anguish and sadness.

On Christmas morning, a knock on the door awakened the depressed old man. As he opened the door, he was greeted by a soldier with a large package in his hands. He said, "I was a friend of your son. I have something for you."

The soldier mentioned that he was an artist and then gave the old man the package. Inside, he found a portrait of his son. Though the world would never consider it a work of genius, the painting featured the young man's face in striking detail. Overcome with emotion, the man hung the portrait over the fireplace, pushing aside millions of dollars' worth of art. He sat in his chair and spent Christmas gazing at the gift he had received.

The painting of his son became his most prized possession, eclipsing any interest he had in the other pieces of art for which museums around the world clamored.

As winter turned to spring, the old man died. The art world waited with anticipation for the upcoming auction. According to the will of the old man, all the artworks would be auctioned on Christmas Day, the day he had received the greatest gift.

December 25 soon arrived, and top art collectors gathered to bid on some of the world's most spectacular paintings. The auction began with a painting that was not on anyone's purchase list. It was the painting of the man's son.

The auctioneer asked for an opening bid, but the room was silent. "Who will open the bidding with $100?" No one spoke. Someone said, "Who cares about that painting. Let's move on to the good stuff."

The auctioneer responded, "No, we have to sell this one first. Now, who will take the son?" Finally, a neighbor of the old man offered ten dollars. "I knew the boy, so I'd like to have it." The auctioneer said, "Going once, going twice...sold." The gavel fell.

Cheers filled the room as someone exclaimed, "Now we can bid on the real treasures!"

The auctioneer looked around the room and announced that the auction was over. Everyone was stunned.

"What do you mean, it's over?" someone said. "We didn't come here for a painting of someone's son. There are millions of dollars' worth of art here! What's going on?"

The auctioneer replied, "It's quite simple. According to the will of the father, whoever takes the son gets it all."[34]

Thus, the neighbor who valued the father's son walked away with the extraordinary. Likewise, we gain access to the extraordinary only through God's Son, Jesus Christ. Because of the Father's love, whoever takes the Son gets it all. Now that helps put things in perspective, doesn't it?

The children of Israel waited patiently—for many generations—for the Son of God to arrive. When that moment finally came, some recognized Jesus for who He was—like Simeon—and praised God. His patience and faithfulness were rewarded. But others missed the Messiah entirely and were shut out of an eternity in God's presence.

As we reflect on the passing of another Christmas Season, let me ask you this: Was there a gift you wanted but did not receive? May I suggest that the best Gift you could ever receive—God's only Son—has already been given to you and the real question is "How are you going to respond to that Gift?"

In a sense, you've been invited to a birthday party. It's Jesus' party, but He wants to give you a present instead. He wants to give you the gift of Himself. Will you take Him?

Father God and Rock of Ages, may I—like Simeon—have the patience and trust to wait on you. For all things come to pass exactly as you planned, in your good and perfect timing. This Christmas Season, may I respond to your Son with open arms, deepening my love for Him. For I pray these things in the loving name of Jesus. Amen.

Personal Study: Going Deeper

Warm-up: Think of a major life event which required you to exhibit patience. What specifically were you waiting for? Why was it so hard to be patient? What did you learn about yourself?

Scripture Reading: Luke 2:21-35

List five things you learned about Simeon.

What was the promise that God made to Simeon? What exactly did God do to bring about its fulfillment?

Referring to verses 28-32:

- What did Simeon praise God for?
- What did Simeon expect Jesus' arrival to accomplish?

What are a few of the most important promises that God has made to you?

- Which ones has He fulfilled?
- Which ones are you still waiting for Him to fulfill?
- In what ways should God's faithfulness cause you to praise Him?

Referring to verses 34-35:

- How did Simeon's prophecy come true in later years? Think of specific instances from your previous readings of the Gospels.

- How might the world's opposition to Jesus impact us as His followers? How should we respond to opposition when encountered?

Continue reading in Luke 2:36-38. List five things you learned about Anna.

- How was Anna's story similar to Simeon's? How was it different?
- What is Anna's response to an encounter with Baby Jesus at the temple?
- What can we learn from Anna's response, applying it to our own lives?

8

The Wise Men's Response: Worship

Matthew 2:1-16

Have you ever noticed how difficult it is to get a bunch of people to agree on something? We, as human beings, have an uncanny ability to look at the same thing and respond in vastly different ways.

For instance, when I say "Jerry Jones," what's the first thing that comes to mind? Among football fans, I can't think of a more polarizing person. Ask five people what they think of Jerry, and you're likely to get five very different responses.

1. *He's a winner.* He's won three Super Bowls at the helm of the Dallas Cowboys. I love him!
2. *He's a successful businessman* with a net worth in the billions. I want to be him!
3. *He's a morally questionable guy* who likes to live the playboy lifestyle. It's best if I steer clear of him!

4. *He's got an ego the size of the Grand Canyon.* He's ruined the Cowboys! Time for Jerry to fire himself as general manager. I can't stand him!

5. *Jerry who?* Never heard of him. Don't know him and don't care to!

So, Jerry Jones. Same guy but varied responses, from love to hate to apathy.

Similarly, as we explore Matthew 2:1-16, we'll witness reactions—both positive and negative—to an encounter with God's Son. In fact, we'll see three very different groups of ordinary men (the religious leaders, King Herod, and the Wise Men) respond in three very different ways to this extraordinary Child.

Before we continue, there are a couple of misconceptions to address regarding the Wise Men.

MISCONCEPTION #1: The Wise Men visited Jesus as a newborn in the manger, alongside the shepherds.

REALITY: The Wise Men likely visited Jesus much later, perhaps by as much as one to two years after His birth.

MISCONCEPTION #2: There were three Wise Men (as noted in the old carol "We Three Kings").

REALITY: We don't know how many Wise Men there were because the Bible doesn't say. (And they definitely weren't kings.)

Establishing the Story's Setting

Let's fast-forward to a time when Jesus was one to two years old, beginning with Matthew 2:1-3.

> After Jesus was born in Bethlehem in Judea, during the time of King Herod, Magi [*ESV: wise men, MSG: a band of scholars*] from the east came to Jerusalem and asked, "Where is the one [*the promised Messiah*] who has been born king of the Jews? We saw his star in the east and have come to worship him." When King Herod heard this he was disturbed, and all Jerusalem with him.

This episode takes place after Jesus is born, during the reign of Herod, who ruled from 37 BC to 4 BC. What's Matthew's point in providing this detail? He wants us to understand that this really happened. It's as historical as the reign of King Herod. In short, this is no made-up story.

Meet King Herod

So, what do we know about Herod? He was the classic Jekyll-and-Hyde character...with an exceedingly small dose of Dr. Jekyll and an exceptionally large dose of Edward Hyde!

- *In terms of the Good?* Herod was a great builder. He built cities, fortresses, and palaces. But he is best known for reconstructing the temple in Jerusalem.

- *What about the Bad?* King Herod was an Edomite—a descendant of Esau, not Jacob—yet he sat on the throne of David. In short, he was not the rightful ruler of Israel. He was appointed "King of the Jews" by the Romans.

- *But it gets worse.* At his core, Herod was arrogant, paranoid in the extreme, and a brutal tyrant. He saw threats to his rule around every corner. To end perceived plots over the years, Herod had his brother-in-law, wife, mother-in-law, and three sons killed.

Knowledge of Herod's brutality extended to the Roman Emperor Augustus, who reportedly said, "It is better to be Herod's sow than his son, for a sow has a better chance of surviving his rule of the Jews."[35] Needless to say, King Herod was rightfully viewed as a cruel, paranoid, and merciless usurper.

Meet the Magi

Next, we're introduced to the scholars, who arrived in Jerusalem from the east. But who were these Wise Men? They were the professors and philosophers of their day, originating from modern day Iraq. Our word *magistrate* is a direct descendant of the word *magi*. They were smart and highly educated scholars trained in medicine, history, religion, prophecy, and astronomy.

Since these Magi thought deeply about life, it makes sense to call them "Wise Men." They were wealthy and highly influential, serving as advisors to the king. While they were not kings themselves, it would not be far from the truth to call them kingmakers.

Once the Magi arrived in Jerusalem, they asked a question. "Where is the one who has been born king of the Jews?" The Wise Men understood Jesus was already a King even as a small child. In short, they knew He was the Messiah promised in the Hebrew Scriptures.

The Magi saw "His star," indicating the arrival of the newborn King. This singular sign was the event that inspired their thousand-mile journey. To have so intrigued the Wise Men, this star must have had an amazing presence in the sky. It must have been so unique—so beyond the scope of their usual observations—that it caused them to wonder if this star was of supernatural origin, serving as a sign from God.

But why was this star significant? As experts in many things—including religion and prophecy—the Magi must have been aware of the prophecy of Balaam, found in Numbers 24:17: "I see him, but not now; I behold him, but not near. A star will come out of Jacob; a scepter will rise out of Israel."

The Magi sought this King based on a prophecy found in ancient Scriptures. With all that they had seen and learned, they willingly undertook a long and perilous journey to find a Child and worship Him.

Can you imagine the Magi's neighbors' reactions when they found out the particulars of their trip?

Why are you leaving? "There's this star in the sky that we want to follow."

So, where are you going? "Well, we don't know exactly."

How long will you be gone? "Well, we're not exactly sure about that either."

What do you hope to accomplish? "Well, we're hoping to find a child and worship him."

Boy, for wise guys, you certainly aren't all that bright, are ya?

Joyful News? Troubling News

The news of the Messiah's arrival, brought by the Magi, should have been greeted with enthusiasm by King Herod and every Jew who heard it. But that was not the case. In fact, it deeply troubled the king, even terrified him. This news sounded suspiciously like the emergence of a descendant of David, who would have a legitimate claim to the throne. It could lead to the end of his reign.

All of Jerusalem was also disturbed by the Magi's arrival and their news of an important birth. King Herod was so unstable that the entire city feared what awful thing he might do in response. When he trembled, the entire city shook.

Yet, how could the arrival of a few magi have created such a stir? How would "all Jerusalem" know about a handful of strangers who arrived in a city of some eighty thousand? Because they likely came in a sizable group. The

Bible doesn't say how many Magi there were. Only that they gave three gifts (leading some to assume three Wise Men). Since these were powerful and wealthy men—traveling about a thousand miles each way (some fifty days)—they likely arrived in a caravan, which carried all of their supplies and provided protection. Some have estimated that the total group numbered as many as three hundred. So, their arrival was a big deal, and everyone in Jerusalem would have known about it. No wonder the entire city was buzzing!

Three Responses to King Jesus' Arrival

Response One: Apathy
Matthew 2:4-6

> When he [Herod] had called together all the people's chief priests and teachers of the law, he asked them where the Christ was to be born. "In Bethlehem in Judea," they replied, "for this is what the prophet has written: 'But you, Bethlehem, in the land of Judah, are by no means least among the rulers of Judah; for out of you will come a ruler who will be the shepherd of my people Israel.'" (Micah 5:2, 4)

Upon hearing the Wise Men's news, King Herod began formulating a plan. His first move was to consult the leading Jewish priests and biblical scholars. He wanted to know the prophesied location of the Christ's birth. These religious leaders were undoubtedly aware of the Magi's arrival and their assertion that the promised Messiah had come.

The experts told Herod that Bethlehem was the place, according to God's Word. And it was only five miles from where they were standing!

What actions did these religious leaders take in response to the reported fulfillment of Micah's important prophecy? Did they stampede the doors to go see the long-awaited Messiah for themselves? Did they plan a trip to investigate the truthfulness of the Magi's claim? Did they call their congregations together and rejoice? Without getting too far ahead of ourselves, let me just say that the answer is no, they did not. In fact, as noted Bible scholar, Dr. Craig Keener, observes, "What is remarkable is that the scribes would know where the Messiah would be born yet not act on that knowledge either positively or negatively."[36]

Let's be clear. Their failure to act was not born out of ignorance. The Jews had been longing for a Messiah for generations, but these religious leaders demonstrated an almost incomprehensible apathy towards this monumental news. They were evidently living in their own little world, pursuing their own agenda, looking out for their own interests. They were kissing up to the king—who mattered most to their ambitions—while dismissing the arrival of the Son of God, the true King of the Jews. They were chasing after the wrong person.

Two young brothers were praying. They were spending the night at their grandparents' house the week before Christmas. At bedtime, the two boys knelt beside their bed to say their prayers. The younger one began praying at the top of his lungs: "I PRAY FOR A NEW BICYCLE! I PRAY FOR A NEW X-BOX!" His older brother leaned over, nudged him, and said, "Why are you shouting? God isn't deaf," to which the little brother replied, "No, but Grandma is!"[37]

Like the little boy who dismissed God and pursued his own interests with Grandma, the religious leaders dismissed God and pursued their own interests with King Herod. They were too wrapped up in their own affairs to care about the miraculous thing God was doing in their midst.

The Jews had waited generations for the Messiah to arrive. And when He finally came, the religious leaders exhibited an almost incomprehensible apathy towards their true King!

Response Two: Hostility
Matthew 2:7-8

Then Herod called the Magi secretly and found out from them the exact time the star had appeared. He sent them to Bethlehem and said, "Go and make a careful search for the child. As soon as you find him, report to me, so that I too may go and worship him."

Herod called a private meeting with the Magi. Talk of the Messiah was a volatile issue, and he wanted to be discreet. Pretending to be devout, he asked for the date the scholars first saw the star. Even then, Herod was devising a plan that would later come into play. By learning when the star first appeared, he could determine the approximate age of the Christ-Child.

After learning what he could, King Herod sent the Magi off to Bethlehem in accordance with messianic prophecy. He instructed them to report back to him as soon as they found the Child, "so that I too may go and worship him." But Herod had no interest in worshiping the One who was prophesied to sit on the throne of David. Rather, he deceived the Magi to learn the whereabouts of Jesus without raising suspicion. Then he would go about removing the threat.

When it came to Jesus, Herod was driven by fear and hatred. He was hostile to the point of violence. Let's temporarily fast-forward to the story's end in Matthew 2:12-16 for context. After visiting the Christ-Child, the Wise Men departed for home without returning to Jerusalem and reporting to Herod. They had been warned in a dream not to do so. Likewise, Joseph was also warned in a dream and fled with his family to Egypt. Finally, in verse 16, Matthew detailed Herod's reaction to the news:

> When Herod realized that he had been outwitted by the Magi, he was furious, and he gave orders to kill all the boys in Bethlehem and its vicinity who were two years old and under, in accordance with the time he had

learned from the Magi. [*Again, we surmise that Jesus is not a newborn, but a child no more than two years old.*]

Here, Herod showed his true colors. Being unaware of the Christ-Child's exact identity, his hostility boiled over into the wholesale murder of innocent children. What is nearly incomprehensible is that Herod sought to destroy Jesus even though he believed—at least on some level—that there really was a Child in Bethlehem who was the promised Messiah! What kind of person thinks he's powerful enough to go up against Almighty God and win? Needless to say, Herod's plan ultimately failed to eliminate the Jesus.

King Herod responded with hostility to the Messiah's arrival, perceiving Him as a threat instead of his Savior. In fact, Herod was so blinded by rage and murder that he chose to do battle with God instead of bowing down and worshiping Him!

Response Three: Worship
Matthew 2:9-11

Let's pick up the story where we left it, as the Wise Men depart Jerusalem for Bethlehem. This is the climax! After months of effort, we learn of their personal encounter with the King of kings.

> After they had heard the king, they went on their way, and the star they had seen in the east went ahead of them until it stopped over the place where the child was. When they saw the star [*had stopped*], they were overjoyed.

The same star that had encouraged the Wise Men to travel from their distant home now guided them to the exact location of the God-Child. This was a miracle in and of itself! In the natural world, stars are used for navigation and have been for millennia. But to an exact house? No. Navigating by stars is good, but it's no GPS. Although there has been much speculation on the exact nature of the star, Scripture doesn't give us the exact "how" of its inner workings. Regardless, the star provided accurate guidance to the travelers, just as God intended.

When the Magi finally arrived at their destination, they were overjoyed! After searching for so long, they could hardly contain themselves. The Greek text literally says "they rejoiced with a very great joy!" They piled on the superlatives to emphasize the depth of emotion they felt.

Now things get really interesting. Concluding the story in Matthew 2:11:

> On coming to the house [*ESV: going into the house*], they saw the child with his mother Mary, and they bowed down [*ESV: fell down*] and worshiped him. Then they opened their treasures and presented him with gifts of gold and of frankincense and of myrrh.

The Wise Men's response to an encounter with God's Son is worthy of consideration for a variety of reasons. First, they didn't just look on the young Child from a distance—as the NIV seems to imply—but entered into the "house" (not a stable) of the Messiah and His family. Because of the humble stature of Joseph's family and the small size of houses in those days, this was a very intimate encounter.

Next, we see that when the Magi came into the presence of the young Child, they fell prostrate on the ground and "worshiped him." Note that Jesus' mother, Mary, was not the object of their worship. God's Son was their sole focus. How amazing it must have been to come face-to-face with the One for whom they had so long searched! But not just that. If they had any doubt about the true nature of the Child, it must have been erased completely when they came face-to-face with Him and fell flat on their faces in worship!

This is powerful. Imagine. One day, we too will see Jesus face-to-face. How will we respond? Tears? Yes! Joyful shouts? Yes! Falling to the floor in worship? Yes! Relief? Yes! Awe? Yes! Comforted? Yes! A sense of pure, undefiled peace? Yes! Plus a dozen other emotions that give true meaning to the word *awesome*!

> One day, we too will see Jesus face-to-face. How will you respond?

Now let's consider the ways the Wise Men *did not* respond to Jesus. Upon entering the house, they *did not* respond with disappointment. After all, Jesus *did not* look like a king. His home *did not* look like a castle. He had *no* scepter, commanded *no* armies, and bestowed *no* fancy titles. To the uninformed eye, He was *nothing* but a peasant child.

Yet to the Magi, this humble Child was the King! Jesus possessed more royalty in His poverty than Herod had in his palace. Somehow, the Wise Men saw beyond the present and into the future. And they worshiped Him! They knew this Child would one day rule both the heavens and the earth, and they were not afraid to fall on their faces before Him.

Think of the contrast. Although the Magi met King Herod, they made no effort to worship him. But when they finally found young Jesus, these educated men fell on their faces before Him. Also, contrast their response with the apathy exhibited by the Jewish religious leaders. What irony!

As a final, tangible act of worship, the Magi presented young Jesus with extravagant gifts of gold, incense (frankincense), and myrrh. This was an act demonstrating His great worth!

In terms of the three gifts themselves, it's been said that the gold was associated with royalty, representing Jesus' kingship. Frankincense was an expensive and fragrant incense, made from the resin of a special tree. It was used in religious ceremonies, representing Christ's deity, as well as His role as our High Priest. Finally, myrrh was an expensive perfume, often used to prepare a body for burial, representing both Christ's humanity and the great sacrifice He would make.

Certainly, the early readers of Matthew's gospel would have been astounded by the sheer value and extravagance of the Wise Men's gifts! But they were gifts worthy of a King and an appropriate act of worship for One so special.

The Magi responded to the One True King by worshiping Him unreservedly! They demonstrated the Christ-Child's worth in an extraordinary way, falling on their faces and presenting Him with priceless gifts, including their time (months of travel), talents (expertise developed over the years through education and experience), and treasure (gold, frankincense, and myrrh).

Learning from the Wise Men

How do you view Jesus? If someone were to take your spiritual temperature today, what would it say about the state of your faith? Are you loving God with all that you are and worshiping Him? Or are you in a dry spell and not feeling much of anything but apathy? Or are you angry with God—separated from Him—and feeling hostile?

I'm reminded of the young father we met earlier, in chapter 4. He received what he thought was an empty box as a Christmas gift from his four-year-old daughter.

He scolded her because he felt it wasn't right to give an empty box as a present. However, what the young father did not realize was that his response to his daughter's gift was rooted in a profound misunderstanding. In actuality, the box contained the best Christmas gift he could ever have hoped for. It was full of kisses that his daughter painstakingly placed in the box herself!

It's easy to miss the priceless presents—those truly precious gifts in life—when we're expecting something different. That's how most people viewed the coming of the Messiah. It was unremarkable, humble, and not at all what the world expected. Yet the arrival of God's Son represented a "box full of kisses" from God!

- The Wise Men saw Christ's birth in this way, as a box full of kisses from God, and they responded with both joy and worship!

But not everyone responded positively to the Messiah's arrival.

- King Herod saw the birth of Christ as a box full of threats and responded with hostility.
- The religious leaders saw Jesus' arrival as a box full of nothing—an empty box—and responded with apathy.

With Whom Do You Identify?

The Wise Men's Response: Worship

The Magi understood Jesus deserved the worship of all people, from kings to paupers. In fact, Scripture teaches that our very lives should be an act of worship in service to Him. In everything we do—public or private—we should glorify God's Son, worshiping Him for who He is and praising Him for all that He has done.

So, let's take a moment to camp on this idea of worship. The word itself comes from an old English word *worthship*. We don't use that word anymore, but we do assign worth to things all of the time. We constantly ask, "How much does that cost?" "How valuable is it?" When we meet someone with a big diamond ring, we might say, "What a nice ring!" But what we're thinking is, "How much is that thing worth?"

In our context, worth-ship is simply ascribing worth to God. It is acting in such a way that we clearly demonstrate His worth to us. When we worship God, it's about more than going through the motions. It is a heartfelt demonstration of our love for Him. In reality, we are to worship God with all that we are in terms of our thoughts, behaviors, decisions, and actions. As we do this—minute by minute, day by day—our lives themselves become powerful acts of worship.

You'll likely find no better time than the Christmas Season to respond joyfully to God's Son in authentic worship.

As you have the chance to recount the amazing stories surrounding His birth, make sure you take the time to dig into them, as if hearing them for the first time. There is nothing more special and unique than the incarnation: God taking on flesh—for the first time and forevermore—and walking among us. This is one-of-one in the Bible. Lean into the joy of the season and worship God!

Herod's Response: Hostility

Maybe you can't identify with the Wise Men's response to God's Son. You're in a different place. Perhaps, like Herod, you're feeling hostility towards God. Maybe you blame Him for some bad things that have happened to you, and you feel separated from God. If so, I've got something particularly important for you to consider.

The Bible says we are all sinners—that is, we've all done things we know are wrong—falling short of God's perfect standard. It's our sin that separates us from God. And because of our sin, we've each earned "death," which is eternal separation from Him.

But God loves us too much to leave us mired in our sin, in a hopeless state. So, He provided a way for each of us to be restored to a right relationship with Him. That way goes through Jesus. By placing your faith in God's only Son, who lived a sinless life and died in our place, the required penalty for our sin is paid. And Jesus was raised from the dead on the third day, conquering death for all who believe in Him. So, have you trusted Him to pay the required penalty for your sin and to save you from an eternity apart from God? If you want peace with God to replace your hostility towards Him, why not trust Jesus as your Lord and Savior today?

Religious Leaders' Response: Apathy

For those of us who have trusted Christ, the Bible tells us we're either pursuing our First Love with passion and commitment or we're lukewarm, chasing after other things, having lost the fire. In short, our faith is characterized by apathy, perhaps like the religious leaders.

But all is not lost if you find yourself in a spiritual desert, overcome with a sense of spiritual dryness. Don't overlook the fact that when we encounter the living God, as the Wise Men did, it results not only in worship but great joy! Is your life lacking joy? Perhaps that's because you haven't had an encounter with the living God in a while. Perhaps it's time to reengage and return to your First Love.

But how do you do that? Jesus Himself tells us in Revelation 2:4-5. Speaking to the church in Ephesus, the Lord said, "You have forsaken the love you had at first. Consider how far you have fallen! Repent and do the things you did at first." So, if you find yourself in a spiritual funk, perhaps you might find this simple approach helpful.

- **Remember:** Begin by remembering who you were before Jesus rescued you from the darkness. Contrast that with who you became after trusting Christ. Can you imagine living life today without the eternal hope you have, as contrasted with the hopelessness and fear that characterized your life before you were saved?

- **Repent:** Own your sins before God. Unconfessed sin can become a wall, keeping us from intimate fellowship with Him. Perhaps you haven't made time for God: you rarely read God's Word, pray, worship, serve, give, or fellowship with other believers. Maybe there's some other sinful behavior—addiction, anger, adultery, arrogance, etc.—that's putting up a wall between you and God. Confess it all!

- **Return:** Reengage and return to your First Love. Do the things that you did when you first gave your heart to Jesus. God is faithful. He will welcome you back with open arms!

Jesus provides great encouragement for anyone seeking to change their spiritual temperature from lukewarm to HOT! Speaking directly to those who are "neither cold nor hot" (Revelation 3:19-20), Jesus said, "Those whom I love I rebuke and discipline. So be earnest, and repent. Here I am! I stand at the door and knock. If anyone hears my voice and opens the door, I will come in and eat with that person, and they with me."

Dear Lord, may we—like the Wise Men—respond to your Son with joy and worship today and every day. May we fully embrace your Extraordinary One, who died for our sins that we might live eternally in His presence: our Savior, Jesus Christ! Amen.

Personal Study: Going Deeper

Scripture Reading: Matthew 2:1-16

Warm-Up: The Wise Men are common fixtures in nativity sets. What surprised you most, if anything, as you reexamined this familiar story?

Why do you think the Magi sought the "King of the Jews"?

How did the Jewish religious leaders respond to the news?

What was Herod's response to news of the Messiah's arrival?

With which group did your response most closely align (Herod, Jewish religious leaders, or the Magi)? Why?

How can you keep focused on the essential elements of the Christmas Season?

Finally, how can you ensure you keep Christ at the center of your life every day, whether Christmastime or not?

9

Postlude: Christmas Year-Round

Perhaps, without realizing it, you've nearly completed a Christmas book deeply rooted in two essential Christ-focused doctrines of our faith: the *incarnation* and the *hypostatic union*. They represent two-sides of the same coin.

The *incarnation* focuses on the reality of God becoming flesh, as the Son was born in Bethlehem. And the *hypostatic union* deals with how His two natures (human and divine) coexist in one Person, Jesus Christ.

Since you've made it this far, let me share some good news with you. You are a theologian. Merry Christmas! In fact, we're all theologians of one sort or another. If you think about God and seek to learn more about Him, then you are "one who studies God" (i.e., a theologian). The only question is whether we are bad theologians or good ones?

Honestly, you might feel that the *incarnation* and *hypostatic union* are just fancy words used by professors and pastors. But let me make a case why you should care too. The truth found in these related concepts encompasses something so special, so unique, and so central to our faith, that it's worth the effort to go deeper. In fact, most of the heresies in the early (and even current) Church centered on the *Person* (the Second Person of the Trinity) and *natures* (divine and human) of Jesus Christ.

So, if you take anything away from this book, let it be the beauty and mystery of the God-Man. When properly appreciated, a new depth and richness will energize your praise and worship, not just at Christmastime but year-round.

God in Flesh: Incarnation

Let's begin by defining *incarnation*.

> INCARNATION (Latin: literally, "in the flesh"): The act of God becoming a human being. This occurred when the Second Person of the Trinity—the Son—was born in Bethlehem. He did not stop being God. And He also took on a full human nature.[38]

Let's restate the truth of our Savior's *incarnation* in language that is both more inspirational and accessible.

When that first cry was heard from a stable in Bethlehem and into the world came the wrinkled, blood-covered Baby, the universe reached a crucial turning point. For the first time ever, the God and Creator of the Universe could be seen and touched! He now occupied human flesh. God incarnate. Approachable. Available. Vulnerable. So amazing and important that words cannot do it justice![39]

Yes, the universe did indeed reach a crucial turning point with the birth of the God-Baby! So, how important is the *incarnation*? C. S. Lewis insightfully writes

The central miracle asserted by Christians is the Incarnation. ... Every other miracle prepares for this, or exhibits this, or results from this.[40]

Noted twentieth-century theologian, J. I. Packer, takes it a step further, noting:

[*The supreme mystery of the Gospel*] is not found in the Good Friday event of Christ's crucifixion, or even in the Easter Sunday event of his resurrection. Rather, the Christmas event of Christ's birth is where the profoundest and most unfathomable depths of the Christian revelation lie. ... Nothing in fiction is so fantastic as is this truth of the incarnation.[41]

In fact, the arrival of the God-Man is not only central to our faith, but even more unique than His resurrection. Let's take a quick survey of the Bible. How many times in all of human history did God become a Man and dwell among humanity? That would be precisely once. How many resurrections does the Bible record? The answer is far more than one.[42]

Now that's not to say that Jesus' death and resurrection should not occupy a central place in the witness and worship of the Church. Because they do and they should. These two redemptive events serve as the bedrock for the conquest of both sin and death. And so we rightly feel a great sense of awe and thanksgiving when contemplating these selfless acts.

Yet the reason Christ's death and resurrection is one-of-a-kind special is not because of a death and resurrection, per se. Rather, it's because of Who it was that died on the cross and Who it was that was raised on Easter. The God-Man.

If it was someone other than Jesus Christ who died and rose, then "we are of all people most to be pitied" (1 Corinthians 15:19). For sin and death would still reign and the free gift of eternal life through faith in Jesus Christ would be off the table. But we praise God that this is not the case!

Believe it or not, the effectiveness of Jesus' death and resurrection is rooted in the *incarnation*. But why must Jesus have been both fully God and fully Human? In order to satisfy the required penalty for our sin, Jesus had to be fully God to be a *worthy sacrifice*, acceptable to God. And Jesus also had to be fully Human in order to be a *representative sacrifice*, having been one of us and experienced the same kinds of things that we experienced.

One Person, Two Natures: Hypostatic Union

Now let's turn our attention to the *hypostatic union.*

> HYPOSTATIC UNION (Greek: *hypostasis*—substance, nature, essence): Referring to Jesus Christ's two natures (human and God) being united in one Person. When the Son became human, his divine nature was forever united with his human nature.[43]

Early believers found this truth so central to the faith that they gathered together and wrote creeds and statements of faith about it. Let me quote key sections of the widely accepted *Definition of Chalcedon* (AD 451), regarding the Person and natures of Christ.[44] Don't get too caught up in the archaic nature of the language.

> [*We confess*] one and the same Son, our Lord Jesus Christ. This same one is perfect in deity, and the same one is perfect in humanity; the same one is true God and true man, comprising a rational soul and a body.
>
> He is of the same essence as the Father according to his deity, and the same one is of the same essence with us according to his humanity, like us in all things except sin.

He is one and the same Christ, Son, Lord, and Only Begotten, who is made known in two natures united unconfusedly, unchangeably, indivisibly, inseparably. The distinction between the natures is not at all destroyed because of the union, but rather the property of each nature is preserved and concurs together into one person and subsistence.

Let's take a moment to camp on this mind-bending idea of Jesus being both fully God and fully Man. First, He is like His Father in every way. Yet, He is also like you and me in every way, except for sin.

Think of the staggering ramifications. God is unreservedly taking part in the same human nature that we possess. As a result, we not only worship a God who created us, but also a God who can directly identify with us! He is both infinite and personal. And that is one crucial thing that makes Christianity unique among world religions.

> God is unreservedly participating in the same human nature that we possess.

Returning to the *Definition of Chalcedon*, the church leaders met to straighten out misunderstandings that had developed about Jesus over the years. Let me use an illustration to help explain the various heresies that they were attempting to counter. Remember, this is as important for us today as it was for them centuries ago.

Assume Christ's deity is represented by the color blue, and His humanity is represented by red.

JESUS CHRIST IS...
- He is both fully blue and fully red simultaneously, united as one, but without mixture.

JESUS CHRIST IS NOT...
- He is not divided into two, being separately blue and separately red.
- He is not just blue (denying His humanity).
- He is not just red (denying his deity).
- He is not purple, representing the mixing of His natures (red and blue) into a third other.

Final Thoughts: The God-Man Year Round

As we wrap-up the Christmas Season—and our exploration of the Messiah's arrival comes to a close—I am reminded that we've been given the most precious Gift ever given. But this special Gift is not only from God. It is the Gift of God Himself. Born on a bleak night to two frightened first-time parents, the God-Baby represented the most wondrous of miracles. God in flesh. Fully God. Fully Human. Coexisting in one Person, Jesus Christ. One of a kind. Never to be repeated.

As we move into the new year, let's not move on from the supreme mystery of the incarnation. Let's seek to maintain the sense of wonder, amazement, and thanksgiving we've developed. Let's commit to giving the arrival of "God in Flesh" the same attention as His death and resurrection. In fact, all three should sit in pride-of-place year-round, at the center of the Church's worship and witness.

I want to end with a quote from Martin Luther, the founder of Protestantism. He manages to capture both the mystery and majesty of the Son's arrival. You can almost feel him worshiping as he pens these words.

> He [*Jesus Christ*] condescends to assume my flesh and blood, my body and soul. He does not become an angel or another magnificent creature; He becomes a man. This is a token of God's mercy to wretched human beings; the human heart cannot grasp or understand, let alone express it.[45]

The End?

He who testifies to these things says,
"Yes, I am coming soon."
Amen. Come, Lord Jesus.
Revelation 22:20

The Next Arrival[46]

Endnotes

1. Entry on "Marriage" from the *International Standard Bible Encyclopedia*, edited by Geoffrey W. Bromiley

2. Matthew 1:19

3. Michael is the other angel mentioned by name in the Bible.

4. The distance, as the crow flies, from Jerusalem to Nazareth is 65 miles.

5. John 1:46 (ESV)

6. Luke 1:29 (NLT)

7. Contrast Mary's angelic encounter with Zechariah's (Luke 1:11-20). He was struck mute when he failed to believe Gabriel's message that Elizabeth would bear a son.

8. Malachi 3:1

9. Messiah (Hebrew) and Christ (Greek) both mean "anointed one." When we say "Jesus Christ" we are really saying, "Jesus the Christ." It is Jesus' title and not a last name.

10. Matthew 1:1-17

11. John 19:25-27 (Jesus' crucifixion) and Acts 1:14 (Pentecost) note Mary's presence.

12. Adapted from an illustration by Roy Fowler from the book *The Gift of a Kiss: And Other Inspirational Stories*

13. The quote is attributed to Suetonius, a Roman biographer who lived in the second century and wrote a biography on Augustus.

14. Although the distance from Nazareth to Bethlehem was only 70 miles, as the crow flies, Mary and Joseph probably traveled closer to 90 miles. The preferred route would have taken them east, along the Jordan River, for much of the journey.

15. Mark 6:3

16. Original author unknown but widely circulated on the internet

17. From the book *Jesus According to Scripture: Restoring the Portrait from the Gospels* by Dr. Darrell Bock

18. From Max Lucado's book *God Came Near: Chronicles of the Christ*

19. Adapted from an illustration by David Laroche from *The Gift of Christmas*

20. Original author unknown but widely circulated on the internet

21. Based on evangelistic training offered by Evantell (Evantell.org)

22. From the book *In the Grip of Grace* by Max Lucado

23. Leviticus 12:1-8

24. Exodus 13:2, 12

25. Numbers 18:15-16

26. Isaiah 40:1-2

27. Simeon's exact words were recorded in Scripture for us to enjoy and study in Luke 2:28-32, which is commonly referred to as "Simeon's Hymn of Praise."

28. *Yahweh-Yireh* (Hebrew) means "the LORD will provide" and is used in response to God's provision of a substitute sacrifice for Abraham's son, Isaac (Genesis 22:14). The King James translation popularized the use of *Jehovah Jireh*.

29. From Dr. Darrell Bock's Commentary on Luke, Volume 1, *Baker Exegetical Commentary on the New Testament*

30. Ibid.

31. John 19:34

32. John 19:25

33. Matthew 25:31-46

34. Illustration by Rick Warren, titled "The Greatest Gift"

35. This quote is widely attributed to Caesar Augustus, but no official record of it exists.

36. From Craig Keener's book *The Gospel of Matthew: A Socio-Rhetorical Commentary*

37. Original author unknown but widely circulated on the internet

38. Adapted from the *Dictionary of Theological Terms in Simplified English* by Debbie Dodd

39. Adapted from a quote attributed to Max Lucado on various websites

40. From the book *Miracles* by C. S. Lewis

41. From the book *Knowing God* by J. I. Packer

42. There are a handful of people who were resurrected, like Lazarus, who

are readily remembered. But there are also an untold number of resurrections which took place, as mentioned in Matthew 27:52-53.

43. Adapted from the *Dictionary of Theological Terms in Simplified English* by Debbie Dodd

44. "The Definition of Chalcedon" (excerpts quoted) was authored by a gathering of church leaders in AD 451 at the Fourth Ecumenical Council. It is a broadly accepted statement about the Person and natures of Christ, affirmed by Protestants (including Evangelicals), the Roman Catholic Church, Greek Orthodox Church, and many others.

45. From Martin Luther's commentary on the Gospel of John

46. We live in an age that anticipates the imminent return of Jesus Christ, which has historically been an integral part of the Advent observance. The birth of Jesus is not technically part of Advent, but rather Christmas. Advent ends on December 24, as anticipation peaks regarding Christ's return...the *Next Arrival*. Most churches have lost this dual meaning, with Advent and Christmas blurring together into one. Here's an interesting tradition that emphasizes these dual concepts, wrapped up in one service. Do you remember Candlelight Christmas Eve services lasting just past midnight? When I was a child, this was one of my favorite services of the year. Shortly before the clock struck midnight, the congregation would light their candles and sing "Oh Come, Oh Come, Emmanuel." This was meant to be a vigil of sorts, as we awaited Christ's return. Then, if Jesus hadn't returned by the time December 25 began at midnight (and He has yet to do so), we'd change gears and celebrate the arrival of the Baby Jesus. We'd typically sing "Silent Night," then blow out the candles, and end the service with "Joy to the World."